THE BUSINESS OF BANKING

THE BUSINESS OF BANKING

Papers and Group Discussions
from the
26th International
Banking Summer School
held at Christ Church, Oxford
July 1973

THE INSTITUTE OF BANKERS
10 Lombard Street, London, E.C.3

Printed in Great Britain at the University Printing House, Cambridge
(Brooke Crutchley, University Printer)

Contents

GROUP DISCUSSIONS:

Foreword

Banking has changed. Earlier generations of bankers would have regarded as revolutionary many of the services that we have today accepted as part of the banks' normal stock-in-trade. And the tempo of change is now becoming even faster.

The 26th International Banking Summer School, held in Oxford in July 1973, provided a timely opportunity to study 'The business of banking' in a world context. What business are the banks in? Where are they going?

This book contains the eight keynote papers given at the I.B.S.S., together with the additional study documents used for syndicate discussions by the bankers from over 50 countries who were selected to attend. The topics covered at the School are so important that all this material is now reproduced for the benefit of everyone concerned with the future of banking.

The Institute of Bankers is particularly grateful to the speakers whose papers form the greater part of this book: their co-operation has enabled us to publish it as soon as the 26th I.B.S.S. ended.

GEOFFREY DIX

Director, 26th I.B.S.S.
Secretary-General,
The Institute of Bankers

July, 1973

The Banking Spectrum

by R. G. Dyson, F.I.B.

It is now 25 years since the first International Banking Summer School was held here in Christ Church, and this our silver jubilee year seems to be an appropriate point at which to take stock of some of the principal developments affecting bankers and banking during the past quarter-century. To those engaged in the busy day-to-day conduct of their affairs the full significance of changes taking place around them is seldom immediately apparent, and it is only in retrospect that a pattern can be discerned which may serve as some guide to the future. The years since 1948 have indeed seen some striking changes, both in the financial environment and in banking attitudes, which could fairly be described as fundamental: the process is by no means over yet, but I hope that when this Summer School finishes at the end of next week you will all feel that at least you have been able to identify some of the likely major developments of the next few years and their attendant problems, and will be all the better prepared to deal with them.

Looking back on the banker's environment in 1948, in the currency world sterling was still the principal international currency. The terms euro-dollar and euro-currency—now so much part of our lives—had not been invented. In the banking world, there were only 7 American banks in London as against some 50 now, and international banking as we now know it was comparatively in its infancy. By and large—and certainly in this country—banking practice still followed traditional and well-defined lines. And that modern 'bogey', the multinational corporation, had barely raised its head. What brought about the transformation which has taken place since then?

The last 25 years

In 1948 the Second World War had been ended three years. Europe was militarily and economically exhausted. The United Kingdom was burdened with debt, and its export industry had been crippled for the necessary benefit of wartime production. The power of the United States was preponderant, and its economy was the only source in the free world to which Europe could look for the means of recovery other than by the laborious process of self-regeneration: in retrospect it was quite inevitable in the circumstances that dominance in the international currency field should swing away from sterling to the dollar.

THE MONETARY SYSTEM

The question of what international monetary system the world should have had of course long been recognized as one of the biggest post-war problems, and it had come under intensive study well before the war ended. There was everywhere a desire for greater co-operation in international affairs, including currencies, as a reaction to the anarchy of the 1930s. In 1944 the Bretton Woods meeting had produced a system involving fixed exchange rates (though changeable in the event of fundamental disequilibrium), freely convertible currencies and freedom of capital movements. However, conditions in Europe and the U.K. in the years following the war made it impossible to introduce the Bretton Woods system in its full form. An attempt to adopt free convertibility of the pound in 1947, following receipt of a large American loan, resulted in a tremendous loss of reserves and set us on the path to eventual devaluation in 1949. The U.K. was forced to adopt means to restrict dollar purchases. Under the Exchange Control Act of 1947 the 'sterling area' was rechristened the 'scheduled territories', and the era of controls introduced in September 1939, as an essential part of the war effort, was continued indefinitely: in fact, with various modifications, it is still with us more than 25 years later.

It was not until 1955 that external sterling convertibility became a reality, and it was as late as 1958 before all the major European currencies became freely convertible for current transactions. Thus the problems of post-war reconstruction were met on our side by controls and restrictions, while the inevitable dollar gap resulting from Europe's demand for American goods which it was not yet in a position to pay for by exports was bridged by the American aid and loan programmes. The best-known item in these was the Marshall Plan which, together with the other aid programmes of the years 1945/51, produced \$17,000 million in non-military grants and \$9,400 million in government loans, about $\frac{2}{3}$ of which in all went to Europe—an example of generosity to potential competitors, and in some cases defeated enemies, which must be unrivalled in history. These programmes had a spectacular effect both in Europe and Japan, reviving their prosperity and restoring their competitiveness in international markets. This competitiveness, coinciding with increased American military expenditure overseas and continued civilian aid programmes as well as an accelerating outflow of direct investment, resulted in the American balance of payments coming under increasing pressure, and the dollar shortage turned into a dollar glut.

STERLING'S DOUBLE ROLE

In 1948, sterling, as already mentioned, was still the leading international currency in spite of Britain's vast expenditure in the Second World War and the loss to our reserves of almost one-third of our overseas investments—worth perhaps £4,000 million at present-day prices—which had been liquidated to help finance these costs. But financing the external costs of the war had, in addition to this disinvestment, resulted in increasing the overseas balances held in sterling in London from £476 million in 1939 to around £3,500 million, of which two-thirds was held by other member countries of the sterling area. The big question was whether Britain's reserves were adequate to provide the liquidity needed to finance the bulk of world trade, as it was still doing in 1948, and at the same time support these enormous external liabilities which were, of course, viewed from the other end, the reserves backing the currencies of the countries concerned. The inability of sterling to fulfill this double role of a trading and a reserve currency was quickly demonstrated by the convertibility crisis of 1947 when the convertibility of sterling stipulated under the terms of the American loan agreement had to be suspended after only six weeks. At this point, the combined adverse balances of Britain and the sterling area on current account with the dollar area amounted to £800 million and, though the suspension of convertibility enabled this deficit to be reduced, it was still over £300 million (which in terms of goods and services represented a good deal more then than it does now) at the time when Marshall Aid came to its rescue.

The history of the subsequent twenty-five years up to the present day has shown all too clearly how difficult it is for any country to carry the dual role of providing both a trading and a reserve currency and it is no wonder that the latter half of that role in particular is now so universally shunned. In the late 1940s and the 1950s the great problem was lack of liquidity. In retrospect it would perhaps have been wiser if Britain had come to terms with its external sterling creditors to fund its debts and repay them over a period, which would have provided much greater latitude for sterling to carry out its role as an international trading currency. However, this is speculation; probably the task in any case would have been beyond us, given the slowness in our growth rate, which has been so disappointing a feature of our economy over this period, for no country can have a strong currency which is attractive to external holders and therefore acceptable internationally unless it is backed by a healthy economy.

THE DOLLAR TAKES OVER

The many problems and restrictions which beset sterling opened the door for another currency to take over its international role and the dollar was the obvious alternative. Not only was it a desirable currency in itself, being backed by the strongest economy in the world, but American policy had, as already described, resulted in its being increasingly available in quantities which virtually eliminated any possibility of a world liquidity crisis.

One result of this outward flow of dollars was the birth of a new term in the currency field, the euro-dollar, a description which does not mean some kind of artificial currency unit but simply a genuine U.S. dollar deposited with a bank outside the U.S.A., including the overseas branches of U.S. banks, which can be transferred freely without regard to any restrictions in force within the U.S.A. Because most of the dollars arising from the American balance of payments deficit tended to find their way on to accounts with European banks, the prefix 'euro' came into existence and has since been extended to other leading currencies when held on deposit outside their country of origin. At first, there was a tendency to regard this apparently new phenomenon with some suspicion but, as realization grew that it was not a rootless book-keeping creation but a real claim on the American economy, its popularity as an international currency grew amazingly. Restrictions imposed by the U.K. on the use of sterling for financing trade outside the sterling area, and at the same time a gradual relaxing of exchange controls and return to convertibility in Europe helped to boost the use of the euro-currency market.

The greatest impulse however came indirectly as the result of U.S. domestic monetary policy and in particular from the famous regulation Q, which put a limit on the interest rates payable by U.S. banks to depositors. Regulation Q was introduced as part of a policy of domestic credit control and was designed to curb the lending capacity of the U.S. banks by making it more difficult for them, at a time of tight money, to raise deposits, but it had the effect of driving the American banks to Europe—mainly London—where they were on the spot to raise euro-funds which they could either send back to their head offices in the U.S.A. for lending there or could lend direct to their international customers in Europe. Added to this were the interest equalization tax, which made it prohibitively expensive for American residents to invest in foreign bonds, and therefore impracticable for European firms to raise money by issues in New York, and other measures restraining American bank lending abroad and American direct investment overseas. These measures effectively helped to transfer New York's international capital market to Europe, especially London, and thus contributed to the emergence of the Eurobond as an increasingly important ingredient in the euro-currency market.

There are now as a result 50 American banks in London at the time of writing and total funds in the euro-currency market were estimated by the Bank for International Settlements to have exceeded $80,000 million by June 1972, $65,000 million of which were denominated in U.S.$. The total is now reckoned to exceed $100,000 million. How much of this has been raised for the benefit of U.S. concerns is not known precisely, but it is interesting and relevant that of the total deposits held by the leading American multinational banks at the same date as the B.I.S. statistics just quoted, nearly one-third, amounting to some $50,000 million, were held at offices outside the U.S.A.

To point the contrast, in 1964 the net volume of dollars in this market was estimated at $8,000 million. This remarkable growth would not of course have been possible had it not been for the persistent American balance of payments deficits which fed the market, and the credit restrictions imposed in the U.S. which deflected borrowers, both in the U.S. and outside, away from New York; but neither would the market have grown so rapidly had it not been for the early recognition in London and elsewhere in Europe that here was a source of funds virtually free from regulation by any national authority, and the speedy development of the sophisticated foreign exchange techniques necessary to make best use of them.

AMERICAN INVESTMENT OVERSEAS

As the dollar gradually came to dominate the international currency scene, so too did the large American corporations extend the range of their interests overseas. They were in any case better placed than others to take advantage of the post-war situation. They had no backlog of post-war recovery to make up, and the rest of the world was crying for their goods. The concept of investing overseas rather than selling overseas was not in itself a new one, but it had particular relevance to the circumstances of the time. During the period of dollar shortage, European governments welcomed the inflow of American capital, which not only provided dollars for their reserves but resulted in the local production of goods which they would otherwise have had to buy from the U.S.A.; and the American government welcomed it too since it was a practical way of getting Europe's recovery off the ground and reduced the need for official assistance. Whereas in 1946 U.S. direct investment in Europe amounted to some $1,000 million, by 1969 it had reached the figure of $21,500 million, with manufacturing companies accounting for $12,000 million and oil companies for about half the balance. At first the larger share of this investment went to the U.K., but during the sixties this picture changed and U.S. investment in the U.K. now totals only about one-third of their total investment in Europe. The whole process was of course enormously helped by the astonishing pace of development in the fields of jet aircraft and of telecommunications, which made it possible for centralised planning and control to be exercised over the activities of subsidiary companies anywhere in the world. It is indeed this aspect of the multinational group above all which, from the shareholders' and managements' point of view, is its greatest asset and, from the host country's, its greatest disadvantage, since it inevitably gives rise to the suspicion that local interests will if necessary be sacrificed to overall profitability.

In a supranational or theoretical sense the concept of a multinational corporation can be said to provide the most efficient use of world resources, but this presupposes a relatively free trade background and a cohesive, not a disjointed, international system. But in the world as it is, the apparent ability of the multinational to take profits where it likes and to switch internal resources internationally as it suits is bound to lead to fears that local national interests will be subordinated to the company's interests or the interests of its country of origin. 'Leads and lags'* in its internal operations can obviously have a marked effect on the balance of payments and foreign exchange reserves of a small host country, and excessive local borrowing, instead of bringing in capital, will diminish local national resources for which there may be other pressing needs. It is possible for a host country to exercise some control over these risks by means of exchange control—local borrowing by foreign companies in particular is frequently restricted—but an effective control requires a degree of sophistication not always available, and then suspicions will remain, notwithstanding the benefits that such companies can bring in the way of know-how,

* Early or late payments in the course of international trade, to take advantage of expected changes in exchange rates.

employment and either import-saving or creation of exports. Nevertheless, whatever may have happened in the past, I believe that most multinational corporations now recognize that to behave as good citizens is, to put it at its lowest, enlightened self-interest, but there is of course nothing to stop them abandoning an investment altogether if it becomes relatively uneconomic in their global plans.

NEW BANKING REQUIREMENTS

The advent of the multinational corporations has introduced a new element not only into world trading but into the lives of bankers as well. The extent of their impact on world trade can be judged by the latest estimates of the value of the annual overseas production of the American multinationals, which is put at $300 billion, and their impact on the banking world is on a corresponding scale. To get the maximum advantage out of a multinational range of subsidiaries obviously involves close control over the allocation and distribution of financial resources, detailed planning in regard to overseas cash flows, and careful assessment of taxation considerations and of currency situations and exchange rates. The corporate treasurer or finance director of the large multinational or international corporation has become very skilled in this task, but it is nevertheless a field in which the banks too will be expected more and more to make a significant contribution towards helping their huge customers with their problems, and this they will only be able to do by extending their coverage in one way or another to all major commercial countries.

Apart from the specialized and demanding requirements of the multinational corporation, the whole range of bank customers and their requirements has expanded, and a host of new services is now expected of a bank. In this country at least there has been in the past a tradition of specialization in financial services, and London's reputation as a financial centre was built up on this basis. With rising incomes and standards of living there has come an increasing money-consciousness on the part of the individual, who now wants a much wider range of personal financial service and does not want the trouble of having to go to several different sources for it. The new banking requirements both of business and the personal customer are to be the subjects of special papers in the course of this Summer School and they will no doubt be dealt with in considerable depth. The big overall question which now faces the banks is whether, or to what extent, they should attempt themselves to supply all these financial services in competition with more specialized institutions.

The Scene Today

Thus the picture in 1973 is very different from 1948. Perhaps 60–70% of the world's trade is now financed in dollars, and the dollar has replaced sterling as the principal international means of payment. While this can now be seen as the inevitable result of the trends already discussed, it is also due to the initiative of those bankers who first seized on the possibilities of the euro-dollar and worked out a technique for using non-resident funds. This has resulted in the nearest approach so far to an international currency which flows across national frontiers and for the time being has virtually eliminated the liquidity problem in international trade. (However, partly for historical reasons and partly because of the expertise developed over the past century in London, sterling still remains a very important trading currency.) The dollar has also superseded sterling as the world's main reserve currency, but in this role it is by no means so popular, as the persistent U.S. payments deficits have created doubts about its own inherent strength, and no one likes being forced to accept it just because, since convertibility was suspended, there is no alternative. The American authorities are well aware of the necessity to rectify their external position to the extent necessary to restore the dollar's reputation, but unilateral action on their part is not in itself enough. Other countries with persistent imbalances, whether debtor or creditor, must also be prepared to co-operate. However, no inconvertible currency can be expected to remain indefinitely in the anomalous dual role of a national currency and at the same time the key to the international system, and the world's leading monetary authorities are making a determined effort, the results of which it is hoped will be revealed at the I.M.F. meeting later this year, to find another sheet anchor.

Meanwhile sterling has given up the unequal struggle to remain a reserve currency and is anxious to shed the role altogether, though in practice this is something easier said than done. There is no anxiety elsewhere to take on sterling's discarded mantle, and to my mind the world will, willy nilly and in spite of the anomalies, remain on a dollar standard for a long time yet.

MONETARY DILEMMA

Nevertheless the inherent dilemma remains that, if the U.S. succeeds in curbing its deficit and restricting the outflow of dollars, which is what its critics would like to see, this might well result in a renewed shortage, or at least fears of a renewed shortage, of liquidity. On the other hand, if the U.S. fails to rectify its own payments position, the world will be faced with having vast resources of an unwanted and mistrusted currency. Pending a more durable solution, which presupposes fundamental changes in attitudes, it seems preferable in the meantime to see the $ strengthened, even if necessary at the expense of the rest of the world's reserves, and to alleviate the danger of shortages of liquidity by a more flexible system of exchange rates. Reserves are needed to meet deficits in payments positions which may themselves arise from—and can certainly be accentuated by—uncertainties about currency values. A more flexible exchange rate system, which will enable adjustments to be made more speedily and thus reduce the period of uncertainty, would certainly reduce the need for reserves. As to what is the desirable level of world liquidity, and whether and how it should or can be related to world trade, is a very difficult question precisely because the need depends so much on the degree of confidence felt about any particular currency or currencies, and confidence is a tender growth very susceptible to changes of climate.

If confidence in the world's reserve currencies, which means confidence in the economies behind the currencies, could be restored, chronic payments disequilibria could be reduced to a much more manageable level. This is the real problem. Unless a currency is fully backed by some completely acceptable and independent asset—such as gold used to be—its value to the outside world must be determined by the world's estimation of the relative value of the goods and services which can be acquired in return for that currency at a given parity. Because this estimation will vary from time to time for a wide variety of reasons, political as well as economic, flexible rather than fixed exchange rates are necessary to maintain the correct equilibrium; the alternative, of endeavouring to maintain a fixed rate when the equilibrium has been disturbed, means the danger of sacrificing the domestic economy in favour of an unrealistic exchange stability, and will inevitably result in the over-compensating stop-go conditions we have experienced here so often in the last 25 years. On the other hand, an unlimited flexibility, i.e. a freely floating rate, may mean that domestic corrections are not made as soon as they ought to be, and will certainly make it very difficult to conclude long-term contracts overseas. The solution must be in wider—and effective—exchange rate bands, and not only a quick appreciation of developing faults in the internal economy but quick action to remedy them, for in the long run a currency can only be as strong as the economy behind it. No exchange rate system, however elaborate or flexible, can be a substitute for sound economic management at home.

A return to gold convertibility, even at a realistic price, seems at present unlikely, though whatever the demerits of gold as a currency backing it probably still enjoys greater and more widespread acceptability than any artificial device, and it is far too early to say that its day is over. S.D.R.s are a useful supplementary form of reserve from the liquidity aspect, as a means of avoiding temporary pressures, but to be satisfactory in the longer term they must have a relatively steady value in terms of the goods and services they can command, that is to say they can be used to settle external bills or make external payments without suffering depreciation. Unless they can be linked to some commonly agreed standard which acts as a fairly efficient store of value, further instability will arise. Basing them on present-day national currencies which are themselves depreciating in real terms would, in turn, bring about a depreciation of the S.D.R., and eventually undermine the whole concept of a managed international monetary system. As yet there is little sign of widespread willingness to look the realities of the situation squarely in the face.

RIVAL CURRENCIES

For the foreseeable future therefore—and foreseeable in a political context is a relative and unquantifiable term—the dollar is likely to maintain its place as the main international trading and reserve currency, for the good reasons that there is no immediate alternative, that at least there are enough dollars in circulation to provide liquidity and that, whatever troubles it may be passing through, the intrinsic strength of the U.S. economy is still enormous. This is not to say that the dollar has no potential rivals. Clearly the yen is a candidate for international currency status, but not until the Japanese adopt a much more liberal trade and investment policy which will increase the supply of yen available to non-resident holders and widen the opportunities for them to use it. At present there are few signs of this, and the relaxation may come gradually, perhaps beginning in the Far East and then spreading its ripples further afield. The resumption of links between Japan and China could be of great significance in this connection. In Europe, in due course the E.E.C. is committed to a full monetary union which logically should lead to a single currency unit or at least fixed rates inside and a single currency policy vis à vis the world outside the Community; but at present its members show no enthusiasm for their currencies or currency assuming either now or in the future the role of an international currency which outsiders might wish to hold for its own sake.

There remains the area of the world dominated by the U.S.S.R., but this is not yet a sufficiently substantial foreign exchange earner and has essential import requirements of its own: in the present decade there is little likelihood of the rouble forming the basis of more than a localized currency bloc. One is left with the conclusion that, though these three currencies will have increasing regional importance, and indeed the bulk of the world's trading may come to be done in one of four currencies on a regional basis—the dollar, the E.E.C. unit (whatever the unit may be called), the yen and the convertible rouble—none of the latter three currencies is likely for some time yet to approach the dollar in international status as a trading and reserve currency. Ultimately one hopes for the day when international accounts will be settled between countries or groups of countries by the use of a supranational unit of account, but this still seems a remote prospect because of the sacrifice of sovereignty it would involve in a world which, the E.E.C. apart, seems more anxious to split into small units than to integrate.

Meanwhile, as the E.E.C. gradually develops its ideal of a

unified financial system, holdings of the currencies of the member countries by other members, at present classified as non-resident or 'euro', should gradually dwindle as they become resident holdings, but the euro-dollar will remain even if it has less importance in the international financial system than it does now. As mentioned earlier, the size of the euro-currency market denominated in dollars was estimated at $65,000 million at June 1972, and must now be much larger. Even if this figure has been swollen by recycling, it must embody a huge external claim on the U.S. economy, which can only be reduced by using the dollars to acquire American goods and services or domestic investments or by liquidating U.S. investments overseas. Such a trend could entail a significant turn-round in the American external payments position which, within reason, would be welcome provided it did not reach such proportions as to precipitate once again a liquidity problem. There seems little likelihood of a speedy change in this direction, and the non-resident dollar will continue to enjoy its important place in international financing.

REMOVAL OF CONTROLS

President Nixon however has undertaken, as part of the dollar devaluation package last February, that certain of the controls which were originally responsible for the development of the London euro-dollar market will be removed by the end of 1974 at the latest. One of these is the interest equalization tax, the others concern American bank lending and direct investment overseas, and I referred to both earlier. A lot can happen before the end of 1974, but if these controls come off it will then be possible for foreign companies to borrow dollars in New York instead of London, and American companies having income arising abroad will be able to remit dollars home to the U.S.A. without any fear that they will then be locked in and unavailable for remittance overseas again if required. This could greatly affect the euro-dollar and eurobond market and much of it could return to New York. On the other hand, the European euro-dollar market is efficient, its ways have become familiar, and on its own merits it may stand up against such influences. And there are to be reckoned with also the enormous revenues of the Middle East oil-producing countries, much of which will no doubt go to swell and eventually dominate the eurocurrency market.

There are those who look on the euro-dollar with some reservations just because it is so free from controls. Whereas in the days before the Second World War, when sterling was the main international currency, there was no distinction in London between resident and non-resident holders and therefore no separate market, the concept of the euro-dollar has grown up as a result of discrimination between resident and non-resident holders. The latter are free to trade their dollars as they like, in a market which is domiciled outside the U.S.A., which is governed by no legislation, and has no dollar lender of last resort. The fear is therefore that if, as a result of injudicious lending, the market was to get into difficulties, there would be no central authority to which to turn for help. Because of this, lenders in this market are more than usually particular about the status and strength of borrowers, and generally speaking the quality of business is very high. Nevertheless it is far from inconceivable that a borrower who had required his euro-dollars for domestic purposes, and therefore converted them into his local currency at his central bank might find that, when he required dollars again to effect repayment, the request embarrassed his authorities. This is particularly so if the original borrowing was taken in dollars partly or mainly to boost the currency reserves of the country involved. Though all central banks worthy of their salt undoubtedly watch the position, the need for some sort of international control—through for instance a body like the Bank for International

Settlements—remains a question which may some day call for an answer.

THE BANKS' CHANGING FUNCTION

In the atmosphere of growing internationalism, immeasurably speedier communications, and increasing sophistication on the part of their customers, the banks of the world have not stood still either. The classical view—held in the U.K. at least—that the function of a bank is to raise money on current or short-term deposit account in order to cater for the working capital requirements of the community—has had to be modified to meet the needs of commerce and industry for longer-term capital on the grandiose scale which modern technology has brought about. The 'conglomerate' and the 'multinational' have introduced new dimensions both in the size and in the scope and geographical spread of corporate requirements, which even the biggest banks find difficulty in meeting single-handed. Nor will direct representation overseas, though essential if banks are to provide worldwide service to and linkage with their customers, necessarily be enough to enable their wants to be satisfied.

The sheer scale of the demand for their facilities has made co-operation between banks, both nationally and internationally, inevitable, and this can be expected to continue. Hitherto this has been achieved mainly through participations in particular loans or credits, or through associations, which may be quite loose, and informal consortia, or may take the form of separate companies in which the associated banks are shareholders. The weakness of these companies is that, if there are several shareholders, all of roughly the same size, with equal shareholdings, the company may lack the positive single-minded direction which alone can give it a corporate personality and growth prospects of its own. Ultimately, though size by itself is not to be equated with efficiency, I think that the solution will be found in more mergers, which may well cross frontiers when permitted, or in takeovers which will result in the formation of international bank holding companies with wholly-owned local subsidiaries in individual countries. Here, however, politics intervene. Domestic control of domestic banking is jealously regarded as essential to financial independence. There is little sign that any major country is prepared to adopt an international outlook on this, but in Europe at least a development on these lines must be implicit in the concept of the Community.

However slow this true internationalization of banking may be to come about, technology should certainly make a much speedier impact on the internationalization of banking services, as for instance money transfer systems. Multinational companies will come to expect facilities to be held available for them in any major commercial country where they operate, and to have a choice of currencies available at short notice, and they will expect such refinements as 'same-day value' for the international transfer of funds. Banks wishing to compete for their business will have to have the organization and equipment necessary to provide these services. On the other hand, the cost of such services and, in particular, the loss of interest on overnight funds on possibly a very large scale if money transmission is greatly speeded up, will be factors on the other side entering into the complicated equation which future bank general managements will have to solve if they are to maintain profitability. Profit-consciousness is just as important for banks as for any other business in a free enterprise world, because the making of profits in a competitive environment is still the most conclusive test of management. From the nature of their resources—that is to say the savings and working capital of the community—banks will always have to pay regard to the quality of their assets and to balance security against profitability. They must also, because they hold so large a proportion of the community's resources, and because these are so important an element in national economic management, pay due regard to national interest and the public's requirements. But, subject to giving appropriate weight to these two considerations, banks are in business to make good profits, and would not be doing the community a good service if they behaved otherwise.

SIGNIFICANT EVENTS

If I were to attempt to pick out the features of the last 25 years which have the most far-reaching implications they would be, in domestic banking, the growing concept that almost anything to do with money is a legitimate profit-earner for the banks and, in international banking, the growing readiness to trade in other countries' currencies. In this country, the self-imposed limitations both as regards the scope of the activities in which it was thought proper for a banker to engage, and the length of the view which it was thought right for him to take when lending other people's money, have been the subject of increasing examination over the last few years, and by no means only from outside critics. Two events of far reaching significance for this country have occurred in the last two years. Firstly, the ending in 1971 of the direct link between Bank rate and the rates allowed and charged by the joint stock banks, and the abolition of the so-called cartel between banks, opened the door to direct price competition between the banks. There had always been strong competition for business between them, stronger than the outside world appears to have thought but, while they were tied as to the rates they could quote, this competition was limited to the field of services and in particular the opening of branches.

One of the most important consequences of this freedom to compete for money has been the expansion of the wholesale sterling market in its various forms. This market was of course no new development and had been—and still is—of vital importance to the overseas and foreign banks, as it gives them the opportunity to raise wholesale deposits and thus overcome the disadvantages of having no widespread branching system. But it had been denied to the clearing banks, who could quote only for funds on seven-day deposit and at an agreed rate. Now the clearing banks are perfectly free to go into this market which they do, not only to raise their marginal requirements for funds, but also to balance their day-to-day positions and to maintain their liquidity. However, the restrictions were removed at a time when money was plentiful and, by and large, as a result of official attempts to stimulate the economy, this situation has remained although official policy is clearly moving into reverse in respect of the money supply. Because interest is itself an element in costs, which must be kept down, but on the other hand is the chosen instrument to be used in restricting credit and therefore must be allowed to rise if necessary, high interest rates have created a dilemma for the authorities as well as embarrassingly high profits for the banks. It remains to be seen how long the free play of market forces will be allowed to operate, but the resources of the banks are such an important element in the economy of the country that one cannot imagine any modern government allowing unrestricted competition to develop without regard to surrounding economic conditions.

INFLUENCE OF THE E.E.C.

The other very significant event is of course the enlargement of the E.E.C., which means that our banking system and principles will have to be harmonized with those of the other member countries. Eventually there will have to be an overall economic policy within which the whole harmonized banking system will have to operate. At present the banking philosophies of the U.K. and Europe differ quite widely. There is far less statutory or regulatory control in the U.K., where the practice has been to leave it to the prudence of bankers to run their own affairs, with the Bank of England keeping a maternal but unobtrusive eye on them from the background. In the U.K., as in the U.S.A., there has always been a conviction that it would be wrong for the banks, because of the nature of their resources, to get locked up in equity investment in industry and commerce and to me this still seems a fundamental premise. It can be argued, in favour of the Continental practice, that it ensures a more systematic allocation of national resources and introduces a valuable element of supervision, whereas the ordinary investor tends to invest only for short-term considerations, does not identify himself with the fortunes of the company, and is not in a position as an individual to exercise any practical influence even if he wants to do so. Against that, it is argued that if the banks were to invest in industry on a wide scale there would be too great a concentration of power in their hands, and an inevitable conflict of interest between their twin roles as investor and lender, particularly as they lend other people's money. It is of course the case that the pace of technological development has made the capital demands of industry—and in particular the energy-producing industries—so large that in the short term they cannot be met out of retained cash flow or from the capital market, and institutional help is necessary, at least for a time. In such cases, however, it is my view that as far as possible it should be done on loan, and that where equity is taken up it should in due course be off-loaded so that the banks should not become permanent investors in industry.

A stronger case for banking participation in business equity can be made in the case of infant undertakings where technical and entrepreneurial skill is present but owners' capital is inadequate to bring the business up to a viable marketable size. It has always been and still is difficult for the small business man to know where to go for capital, and his banker is probably better able to assess his quality than anyone else. A capital investment fund for this purpose, which by its nature would be well spread over a large number of comparatively small projects, would not be large enough to endanger depositors' security, and could do much to stimulate a section of the economy which in the aggregate and in spite of the multinationals has an important contribution to make. However, different views on this whole subject of banking participation have always been held on the continent, possibly because the general public have never hitherto had the same interest in investment as they have here and in the U.S.A., and the banks have therefore had to step in. One of the consequences of the enlarged common market could be the stimulation of greater stock exchange activity and a widening of investment interest, which might well result in the banking system being able to restrict its role in this respect to one of relatively short-term sponsorship which would not put its liquidity at risk.

HARMONIZATION

Clearly harmonization in the banking field will take time, in view of the fundamentally different attitudes of mind. Certainly it has to be admitted that the growth of manufacturing industry in Europe over the last twenty-five years gives no grounds for asserting categorically that the continental system is inferior to our own market-orientated system in making capital available to finance industrial expansion. In Japan, of course, the integration of banking with industry is even more complete and the results have been spectacular, but there are underlying differences of national character and tradition there which make it difficult to draw lessons from their experience which would have validity in the western world. Ultimately a compromise must be envisaged which it must be hoped will combine the best of both systems, but to reach this objective and make it work with the maximum benefit to the Community will require imagination and flexibility as well as discipline. I can only express the hope that, in the context of the control and regulation of Europe's future banking system, harmonization will mean liberalization and that there will be the minimum of bureaucratic intervention.

These two features which I have mentioned—the widening concept of banking functions and the readiness to trade in other people's currencies—point the way to the future. Multipurpose banks doing multi-currency lending are the corollary of the growing sophistication and internationalism of their customers. Nevertheless I think experience will show that there are limitations to the multiplicity of financial functions which a bank can provide successfully under one roof. Insurance, for instance—by which I mean the underwriting of risks, not broking—requires a different approach to the assessment of risk and a longer view on the investment of funds. It would be difficult to imagine the same top management turning daily and effortlessly from the one field to the other. Experience is still an indispensable commodity which can only be acquired with time, and there must be a limit to the absorptive capacity of the trained mind. It is more likely that in the principal fields of financial activity there will not be complete integration, but closer association or grouping, which will enable a joint view to be taken where interests overlap, as they are likely to do from time to time when money is the common stock in trade, even if raised and utilized for very different purposes.

CLOSER RELATIONSHIPS

It is at the level of services and advice that the multiplicity of purpose is more likely to be in evidence. Here a distinction has to be drawn between the individual personal customer or small businessman on the one hand and the large corporate customer on the other. 'Financial supermarkets' in the High Street are not for the latter, whose requirements call for the highest degree of expert financial advice. Hitherto, in this country anyway, this has been the province mainly of the merchant bankers, whose historic role has been to provide a body of highly skilled and specialized advisers who, when their advice is needed, are prepared and able to devote themselves with total involvement to their customers' affairs. There are, however, many signs that this separation of function is changing. The large banks in the U.K. are diversifying into this sphere of activity, and have of course behind them a far greater strength of financial resources than a merchant bank on its own. The relaxation by the Bank of England at the beginning of the year of their rules regarding links between clearing banks and merchant banks is an indication that the Bank visualizes a much closer conjunction in future between the source of advice and the source of finance. Whether this is achieved by closer associations or mergers between clearing banks and merchant banks, or by clearing banks building up their own merchant banking function, the result must be to make the relationship between big corporations and their conventional bankers much closer, and make our system more like the continental pattern.

At the High Street level, on the other hand, problems are unlikely to require the same degree of sophistication. Because of the outlets provided by their branch networks, and their close personal knowledge as bankers of their customers, the big banks are uniquely placed to give advice through their branch managements to personal or small business customers who very often have no one else to turn to; and it is a short and logical step from this to implement the advice by providing the consumer finance—hire purchase, leasing or whatever—or recommended form of investment, for instance through a wide variety of unit trusts specially tailored to a wide variety of needs.

I picture the branch manager of the future as something like a general practitioner in the medical world, someone whose main qualification will have to be that of a skilled diagnostician who knows when he can deal with a problem himself or when he should call in one of his specialist departments. I emphasize the word 'skilled'. Professional skill is the keynote to the ever-widening spectrum of opportunity which is opening up for the bankers of the world, and by the same token is the reason why the I.B.S.S., with the unique opportunities it offers to the rising generation of professional bankers of all countries to exchange and sharpen their ideas, plays and will, I am sure, continue to play an increasingly important part.

The Economic Background

by Russell J. Clark, F.I.B.

The justification for including this subject in the School programme is that we, like everyone else, have to conduct our business in the world as it is, which may or may not be the world as we would like it to be. As bankers, with a strategic position in our national economies, we may, perhaps more than most other business men, be able in some measure to influence the course of events. Either way, whether we are bound simply to accept what is or have the possibility of exerting an influence, we need to know what is in fact going on and where the current trends appear to be leading. Only if we have adequate information and take a sufficiently broad view can we discharge our responsibilities to our shareholders, clients and staff. Maybe bankers have a greater need than the members of most other professions to pause and consider what is happening in the world. Banking affects, and is affected by, the fortunes of every branch of industry and commerce. Both we and our customers have to make plans, often for years ahead, requiring the long-term commitment of big capital funds. To do this intelligently ourselves, or to counsel our clients, demands something more than an assessment of the short-term courses of interest rates and exchange rates.

Moreover, because monetary matters are very much the concern of governments, bankers must keep abreast of political, as well as purely economic, developments. The two are, in any case, closely linked, especially now that economic affairs bulk so large in the policy of every government.

Nor is that all. The typical bank is a big institution whose operations make a significant impact on the whole economy. What a bank does, or neglects to do, may be of consequence to the entire community and not simply to shareholders, employees and clients. Banks have social obligations, arising not only from the nature of their business, but also in many instances from their size. They have the kind of social responsibility that is increasingly being recognized by big corporations of all types.

As I understand it, one of the purposes of the I.B.S.S. is to give those who are fortunate enough to attend a chance to stand back and view their daily work in the light of major developments, national and international. It is scarcely possible to become a sort of 'Renaissance man', knowledgeable in all fields, which is what the competent banker of today really ought to be; but at least we have time to identify some of the things that demand, and will go on demanding, our attention. This very pleasant interlude at Christ Church is not to be regarded in isolation. It should be just a part of a continuing process of keeping abreast of significant trends.

Major Developments

As I have hinted already, though the title given to this lecture is 'The Economic Background', what we have to consider goes far beyond the purely economic. Because the range is so wide, I must of necessity be selective. In making my selection I have concentrated on some really major developments that, though general in themselves, have implications for the management of banks and particularly of their international operations. These developments affect the direction of the main thrust of our activities and the deployment of our capital resources. Some of what I have to say will inevitably have a British bias: it will be for you to make the necessary adjustments and to view the problems to which I refer from your own particular standpoints.

The matters I have chosen for discussion relate to changes in the balance of economic power, one international and another domestic. Internationally, the weight has shifted somewhat from North America to Western Europe and from the West as a whole towards the Far East. Since these movements have been taking place in the context of a general expansion of world trade, they have been more or less painless. They are nevertheless of great significance. Domestically, in many of the countries represented in this School, there has been a steady and persistent growth of the public sector and a corresponding relative decline in the private sector. Since this is an international gathering, I shall devote more time to the former change than the latter, but both are of interest to bankers.

INTERDEPENDENCE

The balance of power, political and economic, has been changing almost imperceptibly for some time, but has been brought sharply to our notice by the dollar problem. For the best part of a generation the world, outside the U.S.S.R. and China, has acknowledged, indeed relied on, the economic supremacy of the United States. Their size, natural resources, industrial power and political stability gave them an unrivalled position, the consequences of which they accepted initially with some reluctance. Having accepted the position, however, the United States abandoned to a very great extent her traditional isolationism, and pursued very liberal policies while propounding the doctrine of interdependence.

For a long time many people, including most Americans, thought of interdependence as just a part of the Kennedy oratory. Even now we are slow to accept it as a reality that renders obsolete some of the policies derived from text-books on international economics. For example, text-book international economics is based on the nation-state, but how real is national economic sovereignty? Has not interdependence made the whole concept of the nation-state something of an economic anachronism? The multi-national corporation is one among many demonstrations of this.

Although the word 'interdependence' was not then in vogue, the designers of the Bretton Woods system of international trade and payments recognized the fact of interdependence, and the operations of the system, not least on the trade side, furthered it. One country's exports are another's imports; a payments surplus implies a deficit elsewhere; there are two ends to a currency change, a devaluation of one means a revaluation of others. These were some of the principles of Bretton Woods. Thus membership of the I.M.F. was an acknowledgement of mutual obligations, even if these were not always fulfilled in practice. The ideal of the founding fathers of the I.M.F., the World Bank and the G.A.T.T. was a one-world system.

BRETTON WOODS

The monetary part of the Bretton Woods system as it operated in practice, if not by design, depended on the economically preeminent position of the United States, for the simple reason that it was based on the currency of that country. The arrangement worked well for a long time. The United States had a comfortably favourable balance of payments on current account: the dollar was in short supply and convertible and, therefore, highly desirable. No one, whether trader or central banker, was reluctant to acquire, and if possible to hold, dollars.

The system has collapsed, and one of the main factors contributing to the breakdown was the change in the economic position of the United States in relation to the rest of the world. For most of two decades after the war the United States were unique. Now, though still first, they are no longer alone.

There have been two sides to the change. On the one hand the demands on the United States, national and international, put undue strain even on their enormous economy. On the other hand, the major industrial countries of Western Europe and Japan have developed their capacities and narrowed the economic gap between them and North America. This they have done to a very considerable extent with the assistance of the United States, who have not only given financial aid, but have also liberally exported their managerial and technical skills. Of course a great deal of the industrial know-how of all kinds disseminated by the United States was accompanied by direct investment, some of which has been, or is thought to have been, a rather mixed blessing to the recipients.

Back in the United States there are not wanting those who decry the distribution of know-how as the 'giving away' of one of their country's chief competitive advantages and, as they describe it, the export of American jobs. This has become one of the battlecries of the protectionists, and has converted many trade unionists, who formerly supported free-trade policies, to the cause of protectionism. Such a view may be regrettable and not wholly accurate; but it is certainly understandable.

It is all the more understandable if one tries to look at what has been happening in the rest of the world from the standpoint of the United States. The countries of Western Europe, not content with improving their individual productive power and competitive position, have banded together to form an inward-looking community—as the United States see it—that has the potential to become a formidable rival to the United States. This Community has entered into preferential trading arrangements, that appear to be contrary to the spirit of the G.A.T.T., not only with a number of its European and Mediterranean neighbours but also with former dependencies of its members, mainly in Africa. Not content with this, the Community has a restrictive agricultural policy that seems to bear particularly heavily on American exports of food. Moreover, Western Europe has been unwilling to act in a way consistent with its changed position vis-à-vis the United States. In particular, those countries with persistent surpluses have not made the kind of prompt adjustments necessary to help the dollar. Altogether, this has been enough to drive the most liberal-minded Administration to abandon its free-trading principles.

JAPANESE SUCCESS

Meanwhile, again from the U.S. point of view, Japan has not only been altogether too successful, but has also been reluctant to adjust to her own success. Her sins are manifold. Protected and aided by the United States, she has risen from virtually nothing to become the world's third industrial power, and in the process has outstripped the United States in many lines of manufacture. Instead of using her growing wealth to enrich the lives of her own citizens, she has employed it to expand her capital equipment and her exports. Given an open market in the United States, which she has exploited to the full, she has not reciprocated either by liberalising her imports or by revaluing her under-valued currency except under extreme pressure, and then insufficiently.

There is, of course, another side to the picture. Neither the European Community, nor even Japan, has been as inward-looking or as illiberal as has sometimes been suggested. Nor, for that matter, have the United States been as totally unselfish in their policies as they would like us to believe.

It is probably not very useful to think in terms of apportioning praise and blame. The sober fact is that, largely due to the shift in the balance of economic power and the accompanying deficit in the U.S. balance of payments, the world found itself with a reserve currency in too plentiful supply and therefore no longer universally acceptable. The announcement in August 1971 that the dollar was no longer convertible into gold altered nothing: it was merely an open admission of the dollar's superabundance.

It was also a formal declaration of the death of the Bretton Woods system, which had been approaching dissolution for quite a long time. Thus for well over two years we have been without a world monetary system, and the inevitable consequence has been uncertainty and instability.

With the advantage of hindsight it seems extraordinary that neither the finance ministers of the major countries, nor the central bankers, nor the I.M.F., had even tentative plans in readiness for the day the Bretton Woods arrangements collapsed. Maybe the fault lay partly with the founders, who gave the impression, no doubt unintentionally, that they had created something permanent, the complete answer to the world's monetary and trading needs. It is, of course, always difficult, even with a single institution like a bank, to get reforms agreed in advance of the actual need. Only in face of dire necessity are reforms actually implemented. Yet, as I have suggested earlier, one of the purposes of our being here in Oxford is to help us to assess the course events are taking so that we may be able to act, or at least recommend action, in anticipation of future needs.

The International Monetary System

With regard to the international monetary system, a clear lesson from the recent past seems to be that, as soon as the present Committee of Twenty have reported, a new committee should be appointed to prepare the way for the next reform of the system.

There is no need for me to rehearse in detail the monetary events of the last two or three years that have led up to the most recent ad hoc arrangements. The salient fact is that most of the major currencies are floating in more or less 'dirty' fashion. In the present absence of system this was virtually the only course open. The general float should, however, very definitely be regarded as an interim arrangement, not a permanent solution.

DANGERS OF FLOATING

The dangers of permanent floating seem to me to be threefold. First, while in terms of the relationship between currencies, a downward movement on the part of one means a relative rise in the value of others, the general trend of currencies is more likely to be downwards than upwards. In this sense permanent floating would hasten the fall in the value of money to which the world is for other reasons all too prone.

Secondly, floating positively encourages a belief in economic independence. The strong desire on the part of almost every government to pursue an independent economic policy is frustrated by a system of fixed exchange rates. Such a system compels countries, in certain circumstances, to apply domestic restrictions or to find other means, such as the expenditure of reserves, or borrowing abroad, to support the rate to remedy a deteriorating balance of payments. A floating rate, on the contrary, at least gives the illusion that the balance of payments can be left to take care of itself—yet it is only an illusion for open economies highly dependent on imports. The advantage of fixed (but adjustable) parities is that they require national authorities to recognize that interdependence is a fact of life and to take account of the effects of their actions on other countries. The absence of fixed parities permits independent policies which can easily degenerate into 'beggar-my-neighbour' economic nationalism.

The third danger to which floating gives rise is the emergence of monetary blocs. Already, early in 1973, there were signs of the threat becoming a reality. When rates are fluid, countries quite naturally seek to tie their rates to the currency of their main trading partner in order to secure a more stable basis for trade. Thus several constellations of currencies may emerge. But the possibility of three or four—one based on North America, one on Western Europe, another on Japan and including the Pacific basin and maybe a fourth on Eastern Europe—is not attractive. Monetary arrangements affect trade, and the two together powerfully influence politics. In particular, one must question the desirability, in political as well as economic terms, of driving Japan out of the Western monetary orbit.

MONETARY UNION

The current situation is, in this respect, further complicated by the ambitions of the European Community to achieve monetary integration, which is, of course, something different in kind, though not necessarily in its consequences, from the monetary blocs to which I have just referred. Some countries, notably Britain, believe that the time is not yet ripe for substantial progress towards monetary union, and this view is confirmed by the fact that the countries concerned are having to impose or tighten exchange controls to keep 'the snake within the tunnel'.

One would have thought that the lessons of last year's experiment would have been learned, but apparently not. The lessons are twofold. In the first place, unless the Community is prepared to isolate itself by exchange controls, it cannot get far with its own monetary arrangements while the world, of which the Community is after all an important part, has no monetary system and is consequently subject to frequent disturbance. The members would be better employed contributing with one voice to the discussion in the Committee of Twenty. It is pleasing to note that at the end of March they were beginning to do so, and were putting forward concerted proposals that appeared to fit in with some of those made by Mr. Shultz at the 1972 meetings of the I.M.F.

But the second lesson is that, even when a new world monetary system is in place, monetary union in the Community will not be possible without a common, single centre of decision and a harmonization of many aspects of economic and social policy that are as yet uncoordinated. In other words there will have to be a withering of the nine nation states or the Community will remain a customs union. My own personal view is that this is what ought to happen. Monetary union would then be the natural outcome of political integration. To attempt to reverse the process is to invite division rather than unification.

REQUIREMENTS FOR REFORM

For the reform of the world monetary system there seem to be two fundamental requirements. A new base is necessary which should not be a national currency. Since gold is now something of an anachronism, S.D.R.s, duly modified to eliminate the element of borrowing involved in their present form, seem to be the most reasonable choice. The use of S.D.R.s, in turn, would imply a considerable strengthening of the I.M.F., taking it a big step further in the direction of becoming a world central bank. Of course, as is well understood, a central bank is a powerful institution. A world central bank implies a certain pooling of national sovereignties—hence the hesitation on the part of national governments. However, whether or not the S.D.R. route is taken, an acceptable reserve asset has to be found. We cannot continue indefinitely with a system based on nothing in particular.

A strong I.M.F. is, in my judgment, essential if there is to be any hope of a return to the one-world ideal of Bretton Woods. Hitherto, this ideal has only approached realization when there has been one undisputed economic power whose currency was the basis of the system. For a long time Britain was in the position of leadership and the world was on the so-called gold standard, which was really the sterling standard. In the inter-war period that system broke. Then for a quarter of a century following the second world war, the United States took the place formerly occupied by Britain, and the dollar replaced sterling. Now, with the decline of the dollar and the lack of any other national currency, or group of currencies, to replace it, we appear, in the monetary sense at least, to be moving into a situation analagous to the thirties.

The dollar, of course, remains, and will remain for a long time, the main international reserve asset, but the authorities of the United States would like to see an end to this role and there is no other country whose currency could conceivably replace the dollar. No other country is in a position to support a reserve currency even if it wished to do so. Thus I come back to my insistence that a reserve asset issued by a strengthened I.M.F. is vital to the health of the monetary system, and hence of world trade.

The second basic requirement, which is in a way even more urgent, is a funding of the excess dollar balances in non-resident hands. Technically this is not an insuperable problem, but it is politically difficult and demands an initiative on the part of the U.S. One suggestion is that the U.S. should make a special issue of three- or four-year securities, with an exchange rate guarantee and with an attractive rate of interest. These securities, which would be offered to official holders of dollars, would be repayable on demand but with the provision that interest would be forfeited if they were cashed before maturity.

No doubt there are other more or less ingenious ways of stabilizing the dollar balances, and thus checking the big surges of short-term capital that have proved so disruptive of late. Until something of the kind is done it is idle to talk about restoring the convertibility of the dollar. The alternative is to wait for the United States to achieve a sustained balance of payments surplus which, in spite of all the parity changes that have taken place, still looks a somewhat distant prospect, even after allowing for a rapid growth in their return on overseas investments and other non-trading income.

A POLITICAL QUESTION

One further point may perhaps be made about the reform of the world monetary system. Although there are many difficult technical problems to be solved, the question is fundamentally political. Each country represented in the Committee of Twenty has its own ideas as to the solution that would best suit its own interests. There are divergences of view between the two sides of the Atlantic, between Europe and Japan, and between the United States and Japan. Even within Western Europe a single voice has only just begun to be heard. Moreover, the interests of industrialized countries do not by any means coincide with those of the developing nations. As a digression one may perhaps add the further complication that very few governments, if any, have for long maintained a consistent view of the kind of system they require, though the French are, perhaps, an exception to this generalization. For example, Mr. Barber's current attitude to floating would certainly have disqualified him from the office of Chancellor of the Exchequer in any previous Tory administration. Similarly the approach of the United States to convertibility is now very different from what it was in the early post-war years, when a $1,000 million loan was made available to Britain on condition that the pound was made immediately convertible, a condition that was kept for about six weeks, which was the time needed to spend the loan. Circumstances quite evidently alter cases.

All this means that the recommendations of the Committee of Twenty will be a compromise that will not satisfy any government entirely. As bankers, however, we should judge the outcome by the extent to which it facilitates the international flow of trade and payments. Arrangements, however elegant, that fail on this criterion will not meet the most important need of the world economy. Meanwhile, however hopeful we may be of a rational solution, our contingency planning ought to allow both for a long period of uncertainty and for the emergence of blocs separated by controls.

INFLUENCE OF THE OIL PRODUCERS

So much for the reform of the monetary system. There is, however, another shift in the balance of economic power that constitutes a threat to monetary stability. I refer to the mounting financial resources of the oil countries. The industrial world faces an energy shortage. This does not mean that there is, or will be over the next few years, an insufficiency of energy resources in the absolute sense. Rather it means that all the major industrial countries are dependent on imported supplies, principally of oil, and will continue to be so for many years to come. Nothing that they can do to develop new sources can be of help for a long time. The oil-producing countries have not been slow to realize this and to use their bargaining power. Prices have risen greatly and the end of the rise is not in sight. As I write I have on my desk a copy of *The Economist* bearing the title 'Stand by for dearer oil'.

Apart from the obvious impact of the price of oil on manufacturing costs all over the world, there are two other consequences, both of which are significant for the monetary situation. It will, in the first place, make a reduction of the U.S. deficit, or the achievement of a surplus, more difficult. This point needs no elaboration here.

Secondly, unless the oil-producing countries change the way in which they handle their surpluses, their growing revenues will constitute a growing threat to monetary stability. With their small populations, most of these countries have relatively little scope for increasing their current expenditure, and so their reserves, official and private, accumulate year after year, and their practice so far has been to invest these abroad, primarily in short-term, readily transferable assets. A deposit account seems to be not untypical. Since their revenue is derived from a wasting asset it would surely be in their own interest to find employment for their surpluses in real, rather than purely financial, investments. It would certainly be for the good of the monetary system if they were to do so. Big liquid reserves ready to move instantly in response to interest rate changes, or the prospect of a revaluation, or devaluation, do not make for stability.

The Balance of Economic Power

Having thought about shifts in economic power that have already occurred, what can we say about further changes in the balance? At the risk of being controversial, let me say that there are grounds for arguing that the countries on both sides of the North Atlantic may well have passed their peak in relation to the rest of the world. This is not to say that I expect to see an absolute decline in North America and Western Europe, but simply that rates of economic growth are far greater in a number of other places. Though recent rates of growth of some of these other areas may be unsustainable, they appear to have every chance of going faster than the mature industrial economies for a long time. The development of the E.E.C., assuming that it surmounts its present difficulties, may delay the relative decline for the countries within its borders; but that is all.

The more or less closed economies of the U.S.S.R. and her associates, and of China, are difficult to assess. Clearly their potential is vast, and already attention, even on the part of the United States, is being turned in their direction. Trade missions to these countries are now the 'in' thing, and no doubt profitable exchanges of goods and services will increase. Most of the great continent of Africa has a long way to go; but Latin America, with its natural resources largely untapped and an increasingly sophisticated population, is coming along rapidly.

JAPAN

The real pace-setter, however, is Japan. Without natural

resources, but with a skilled, unified and dedicated people, she has already worked miracles and we have not seen the end of them.

Moreover, one has only to look at her position on the map to see that, potentially at least, she is lacking neither in markets nor in reserves of manpower. Already Japan is supplementing her trading relations with overseas investment. Some of Japan's labour-intensive manufacturing industries are transferring their operations to other parts of the area, notably to Taiwan and Korea. Such direct investment, backed by efficient management, will be, if experience elsewhere is anything to go by, a very powerful force for development in the recipient countries. The whole region is, as we know, rich in natural resources.

Nor is Japan looking only to neighbouring countries for investment opportunities. Manufacturing plants are being established in North America and in Western Europe, mostly on a fairly small scale but often representing big names. Thus the stimulus given by the presence of Japanese enterprise may not be limited to the less-developed areas. An executive of a new Japanese establishment in the north of England was quoted in the *Financial Times* as saying that he believed 'in five years' time our British workers will match Japanese standards'.

Being a surplus country with big financial reserves, Japan is quite properly thinking in terms of lending abroad. Switching from being an international borrower to being an international lender raises both institutional and psychological problems, as Britain found in the years after the war when it was necessary for London to make a change in the opposite direction. A considerable amount of liberalization of laws and attitudes will be required. Though the process may take time, Tokyo undoubtedly has the potential to become, not merely an important regional capital market, but also a truly international centre in competition with London and New York.

After adding up all the assets of the Far East, including scientific and technical skills, which are no longer a monopoly of the West, is it fanciful to suggest that before long the countries of the Pacific basin will need the North Atlantic countries less than the North Atlantic countries need those of the Pacific? Much has been said recently about the need for Japan to restructure her economy if the real benefits of her advance are to be enjoyed by the Japanese people. But perhaps there is just as much restructuring to be done in North America and Western Europe as in Japan if we in the West are to stay in the competitive race or, better still, engage in fruitful collaboration.

INTERNAL CHANGE

So far I have been talking about international shifts in the balance of power. There are, however, changes of balance within the majority of industrial countries of which we must take account in our planning for the future.

First there is the much-discussed question of the quality of life—the worry about pollution in its widest sense. The focus of concern varies from country to country as well as over time. Contamination of coastal resorts by oil discharged at sea, the possibility of some species of wild-life becoming extinct, the threatened exhaustion of essential raw material and energy resources, the excessive size of road transport vehicles, the spoiling of the countryside by urban development—all these things, and many more besides, attract attention, and overriding them all is the pressure of a rapidly expanding world population.

All kinds of philosophical, and even moral, issues are involved in the concern with pollution. Consideration of these would take us far beyond the scope even of this wide-ranging lecture. We should, however, note that the implementation of anti-pollution and preservation policies will mean a very considerable redeployment of resources which, in turn, implies heavy capital expenditure. If at the same time there is a revulsion against the pursuit of growth on the part of young people in some major countries, including Japan, the generation of the necessary funds may present added difficulties. In other words, here is another possible source of inflationary pressure.

CAPITAL HUNGER

It certainly looks as though, whether or not the world continues to make economic expansion one of its principal aims, capital hunger will remain endemic. This suggests that interest rates are likely to stay well above the levels that we used to think of as normal, even if collectively we are successful in checking the rate of inflation, about which it is not easy to be an optimist.

The world-wide demand that preoccupation with quantity should give way to concern about quality is likely to give further impetus to another change of economic balance to which I must refer. In all our countries there has been an increase in the size of the public, as compared with the private, sector. The borderline between the two sectors of the economy may be moved marginally from time to time as governments change, but generally speaking the growth in the public sector that has taken place is irreversible. Indeed, the public sector is likely to make further advances in most places. Certainly the experience of the present government in Britain seems to confirm this.

Mr. Heath, when he came into office in 1970, had the firm intention of reducing the extent of the government's involvement in the economy; but he has been compelled by events to increase it. At the time of the government's discussions with the two sides of industry last year, when there was still hope of a voluntary prices and incomes policy, Mr. Heath made proposals for a partnership between the government, the Confederation of British Industries and the Trades Union Congress in the management of the economy. This was put forward not as a temporary expedient but as a permanent arrangement.

Aside from the irresistible demands of the welfare services, which are in themselves major industries and big users of capital, governments find themselves pulled willy-nilly into activities on the fringe of private industry. They may feel bound to employ public money to support research and development or, as has the British government, to rescue ailing companies deemed to be of national importance. Nor is the British government alone. The wisdom of some of these interventions may be debatable; but there are undoubtedly many projects which, without government backing, would simply not be undertaken. The space programme in the United States, the Concorde, and the proposed Channel Tunnel, are clear examples of projects requiring capital expenditure beyond the capability of private enterprise. They also have this in common, that their merits cannot be determined by normal business criteria. At the same time every project of this kind affects the regional and sectoral distribution of resources and the prosperity, or otherwise, of corporations in the private sector.

THE AID PROGRAMME

Another kind of expenditure in which governments are of necessity involved is, of course, aid to the less-developed countries. All I can say about this is that without question aid, in all its forms, is at present hopelessly inadequate and ought to be increased. To the hard-headed let me add that, as with the space programme and projects of like nature, there is a spin-off for the private sector, including the banks.

This shift of balance in the relationship of the public to the private sector means, I believe, a re-thinking of a good deal of our economics. One of the difficulties in combating inflation seems to me to stem from the fact that the authorities in some countries at least have applied measures that might have been appropriate to a free-market economy but which are inadequate for the kind of mixed economies that we have today. The public sector, which may be 40%, 50% or more of the total, is not responsive to monetary or fiscal measures. Thus, when these are employed, their impact is almost exclusively on the private sector, and the response of the economy as a whole may be disappointingly small. More direct, interventionist, measures are needed. Maybe statutory prices and incomes policies are not as temporary as we sometimes suppose.

These things may offend our free-market principles, but, on the whole, given the irreversibility of the trend in relationship between public and private sectors, we as bankers have more to gain than to lose by collaborating with the authorities. If one may judge by results in Japan, where this kind of approach has never been in question, the outcome is not necessarily disaster.

Conclusion

In conclusion, let me emphasize that I have not attempted a comprehensive survey of the economic background. Much else might have been said. I have tried to make two main points. The first is that, whether we like it or not, international interdependence is a fact of life. This, however, impinges on national sovereignty and provokes resistance often in the form of defensive restrictions on trade and payments. My second point is that, both internationally and nationally, there has been a shift in the economic centre of gravity. On a world scale there is a pull towards the east: domestically, the public sector has acquired a significance that is all too often unrecognized. Whatever we may think about them, there are developments that we as bankers must take into account in planning for the future.

Finance for Industry and Commerce

by Hans Strasser

From family concern to public company

HISTORICAL BACKGROUND

One of the most interesting phases in the history of a company is the stage where the members of a family who have been the sole owners decide to widen the capital base of their company by issuing new shares to the public. The motives behind such a decision are usually based on a number of factors often connected with the trend towards economic concentration. I should like to mention some of the more important ones.

Firstly there are technological considerations: with the lowering of customs barriers and the emergence of huge international markets, industrial corporations are not only exposed to keener competition, but must also be in a position to cope with larger orders. In order to remain competitive they are forced to rationalize their flow of supplies and their sales. All these tasks call for extensive investments in modern machinery and equipment. Furthermore, an aggressive marketing strategy on an international level is likewise costly. Finally, smaller companies as well are obliged to reserve considerable sums for research and for the industrial application of newly-created products. All these investments usually go far beyond the possibilities of small and medium-size firms.

During the past two decades the climate for the development of small- to medium-size companies has been particularly favourable in Switzerland. However, these companies are now faced increasingly with mounting obstacles such as labour shortages, lack of experienced management, and a profit squeeze on the one hand, and by rising investment needs which by far surpass the possibilities of self-financing available on the other. As a result, this category of firm is faced with risks that are no longer in line with the concept of a family business.

ROLE OF BANKS IN GOING PUBLIC

In finding the optimal solution with respect to the new structure of these small- to medium-size companies, the banker plays a decisive role both as advisor and as provider of funds.

The Swiss banker's connections and contacts with most industrial sectors enable him to assist these companies. Thus a real need was met when a few years ago a number of large commercial banks organized special new departments to assist their clients by giving them specific advice in cases of mergers, acquisitions, and the establishment of finance plans tailored to fit individual requirements. To put it in a nutshell, these departments fulfil functions similar to those of the traditional English merchant banks.

As you know, in the United States small corporations that are not yet ready to go public may, when in need of capital quickly, elect to issue securities exempt from registration or regulation by the Securities and Exchange Commission. Under one provision, securities are offered to residents in one state only and can be transferred or sold only to residents of that state. Another avenue is to offer the securities to a limited number of sophisticated investors (usually no more than 20). Here there are no geographical limitations. In order to gain exemption, the securities are sold with the agreement that they cannot be resold without registration or before the elapse of at least two years. To signify his agreement to this provision, the investor usually signs a letter to this effect; stock offered in this manner is therefore called 'letter stock'. It is usually sold at a discount in relation to freely tradeable securities to make up for the lack of marketability. The discounts normally run from 20 to 50%.

In Switzerland private placements in this particular form are not customary. However, small- and medium-size companies have other means at their disposal of widening their capital base. There are a number of finance companies willing to provide the necessary long-term capital without the borrower losing his independence. The large Swiss commercial banks are particularly well placed to establish the necessary connections, as they control holding companies specializing in this type of transaction and with the necessary standing to refinance themselves in the market in case of need. In Switzerland there is also a holding company with bank participation that specializes in providing funds for companies whose shares are not quoted on the stock exchange.

Finally, the Swiss banks play a major part in facilitating access to the capital market for corporations fulfilling the necessary conditions. On the public capital market the borrower has the choice of obtaining long-term funds either in the form of bonds or shares. As in most cases the primary purpose is to reinforce a company's own means, i.e. to obtain additional capital, the first contact of a growing company with the capital market will be to launch a share issue. Here again the procedure to be followed will consist of different stages, the first being an issue on the secondary market. As a rule, once a company has placed part of its shares among a wider public and has thus become sufficiently well known, it may eventually be possible to tap the market by means of a bond issue.

To obtain access to the public capital market, the potential borrower has to fulfil a certain number of conditions which many companies find difficult to comply with: the publication of consolidated balance sheets over a number of years, record of an adequate dividend policy, presentation of annual reports, periodic information on the state of business etc. It cannot be stated often enough, and it is the banker's duty to point this out to his client, that it is pointless to have shares quoted on the stock exchange purely for reasons of prestige. Companies must really be willing to open their business to the public and allow their shares to be traded regularly, thereby taking into account that the shares will be subject to price fluctuations which in turn will have certain fiscal consequences for the shareholders.

In cases where a client company is considering revising its structure by way of merger, it is also the banker's duty to urge that the planned merger should not have an adverse effect on what you might call the net financial position of a given industry. In my opinion it is important that mergers do not result in a reduction of the capital investment in that sector. In other words, in cases of mergers and acquisitions it is desirable that the shareholders of the company that is being absorbed by a larger one or by a whole group are not paid in cash, but receive shares of the company or group buying the smaller one. This method also has a psychological element as it underlines the confidence of the seller in the success of the new company.

REGISTERED STOCK AS A MEANS OF RETAINING AND PROVING SWISS OWNERSHIP

Of course, making part of a company's stock available to a broader circle of shareholders or even the general public may pose the problem of keeping effective control of the company in the hands of the original shareholders. The situation is particularly difficult in Switzerland, where on the one hand the average size of such companies is relatively modest, and on the other the potential demand on Swiss stock markets, fairly high. Within certain limits there are legal provisions facilitating retention of control by the old shareholders. One is the possibility of issuing special preferred shares for the founders, usually in registered form. These shares must be paid up in full and have the same voting rights as the ordinary shares, but can have a par value several times less than the latter. For example, the preferred shares could be issued at a par value of S.fr. 100 (the minimum required by law) and the ordinary shares at S.fr. 500 or S.fr. 1,000, both categories of shareholders having one vote per share.

Another possibility favoured especially by companies wishing to prevent foreigners from gaining control is the creation of registered shares with limited transferability. In this case registrations in the share register of the company can be refused either on grounds specified in the articles of association of the company or without giving any reasons at all. In the course of the last few years a number of Swiss corporations introduced such special registered shares.

Another possible way for a public company to increase its capital without changing the majority rights of existing shareholders is to issue participation certificates. The owners of such certificates are co-owners of a corporation, but have no voting rights and thus no means of influencing the policy of the company concerned. Compared with bond issues, participation certificates have the advantage for the company that they represent no burden as regards fixed interest and repayment obligations.

While the banks fully appreciate the motives behind the sometimes complicated procedures companies employ to ensure the retention of Swiss ownership, they are of course anxious to secure the best transferability possible for these registered shares. In view of this there is an agreement between the banks and the respective corporations under which the banks only apply for registration of new shareholders if satisfied that they fulfil the necessary qualifications. In exchange, the corporations inform the banks of the conditions required for the registration and undertake to complete the necessary registration formalities as quickly as possible.

Financing by capital increase

A Swiss corporation with the necessary qualifications, intending to make use of the capital market for the issue of new shares to the public, contacts one of the leading Swiss banks able to provide the necessary underwriting and syndicating facilities. Whereas in the United States this service is provided by the large investment bankers and in the United Kingdom by special issuing houses—essentially the merchant banks—the Swiss banks have several long-established and well-functioning banking syndicates for the underwriting and sale of new shares and bonds.

The issue of new shares by a Swiss corporation usually takes place in the form of a rights issue. Under Swiss law the shareholder has a right to subscribe proportionally to the new equity capital issues, unless the company's by-laws or a special decision taken at a general stockholders' meeting overrules this right. In practice, shareholders are only asked to renounce their right if new shares of their company are issued for mergers or acquisitions, or if new stock has to be reserved for holders of convertible bonds.

Under these circumstances, a capital increase in Switzerland is viewed as more than a means of raising new capital. Traditionally it has also been a vehicle allowing the shareholders to participate in the company's growth. Whilst a shareholder owning the necessary number of shares may subscribe on favourable terms for new shares, a new investor is required to acquire subscription rights from an existing shareholder willing to sell if he wishes to become a shareowner; in other words, he has to pay the existing shareholder a price for his participation in the now diluted total equity capital and in the growth of the company. In order to facilitate the distribution of shares, the leading Swiss banks, underwriting and syndicating equity issues provide a ready market for subscription rights during the subscription period, which usually lasts about ten business days.

This 'Swiss' system of capital increase practically precludes the issue of new shares at their market price or very near to it. This is also the reason why long-term investors readily accept very low yields for Swiss shares if they buy on the market. With a few exceptions, listed Swiss shares yield between 1% and 3% even for companies with mediocre growth records. However, these companies increase their capital from time to time by issuing new shares at par value or with a relatively modest premium on par value, but considerably below the market price. If the dividend rate is maintained, which is usually the case, the yield on the new shares is very favourable. As a rule it is rarely under 6%, and it may easily exceed 10%. The long-term investor, taking into consideration the total cost of his investment after a number of years, may thus obtain a declining average price per share and a yield comparing favourably with those offered on foreign markets where new shares are usually offered at prices near their latest stock exchange quotations. This is particularly true in the United States.

The system of rights offerings, as well as the fact that the major part of the outstanding shares of Swiss companies must be registered in the name of a Swiss citizen or resident, are the main reasons why Swiss shares are, with a few exceptions, not listed outside Switzerland. If new shares are offered on favourable terms, most of the existing shareholders participate in full by putting up the necessary funds, or they sell only a few subscription rights to finance the acquisition of new shares. This renders the enlargement of the existing circle of shareholders more difficult, and consequently does not warrant an expansion on foreign capital markets. Moreover, the Swiss banks have always attracted custodian accounts of foreigners who may also buy Swiss shares directly in Switzerland and keep them there, where they have a ready daily market. Thus Swiss companies have many foreign shareholders without listing their shares abroad, where they would have to pay considerable listing fees without getting the benefit of an active market.

At present foreigners are not allowed to buy Swiss shares above the total they already owned before June 1972, at which time this measure was introduced as part of the Swiss Federal Government's effort to counteract inflationary pressure in Switzerland.

Summing up the procedure followed in Switzerland for new issues of capital, I should say that the same pattern is followed in most cases. The issue of so-called preferred stock, or the offering of stock options or warrants as they exist in the United States, is still very rare in Switzerland. The most significant difference between the Swiss and the Anglo-Saxon new issue business is that in my country the leading banks are the intermediaries between the borrower and the market, whereas both the United States and the United Kingdom have special institutions for this service. However, this may change, especially in England, where the U.K. clearing banks have now been given an indication by the Bank of England that no objection would be raised should a takeover of a merchant bank be contemplated. This would give the clearing banks a much closer link with commercial and industrial enterprises. Now that the United Kingdom is a member of the European Community, this trend may well be accelerated.

The bond market as a source of finance for industry and commerce

Owing to the high rate of individual and corporate saving, an efficient bond market has developed in Switzerland. As the degree of self-financing of industry and commerce is fairly high, the bond market has traditionally been mainly a means of covering the long-term capital needs of public authorities (Confederation, Cantons, Cities and Municipalities), public utilities (chiefly hydro-electric power stations), and banks (chiefly for financing their mortgage business).

A statistical breakdown of users of the Swiss domestic bond market shows that in 1972, for instance, the three above-mentioned categories accounted for a total of S.fr. 3,818 million out of S.fr. 5,016 million, or nearly 76% of the total value.

The large industrial and commercial concerns have managed to finance their long-term investments to a large extent from internal cash flow, i.e. without tapping the bond market. However, in 1971, industry and commerce borrowed more funds on the capital market than they had previously, and more than in 1972. This can be clearly seen from the following table (the figures refer to new issues, including refunding operations):

(1) Year	(2) Total domestic issues (in S. fr. million)	(3) Total bond borrowings by industry and commerce (in S. fr. million)	(4) (3) as a percentage of (2)
1960	924	24	2·6
1965	2,870	276	9·6
1966	3,014	109	3·6
1967	3,401	36	1·0
1968	2,989	290	9·7
1969	3,336	186	5·6
1970	3,707	63	1·7
1971	5,432	761	14·0
1972	5,016	380	7·6

The 1971 figures are obviously unusual compared with those of the previous years. Indeed, they are exceptional if we look at the 1972 figures, where the industry and commerce share dropped back to 7·6%, out of a total of S.fr. 5,016 million. The question now is what will happen in the future. This will depend upon two factors, namely the extent to which industry and commerce will be able to finance their investments with their cash flow, and the amount of funds that will be made available to this category of borrowers by our capital market, considering that it is subject to a permanent control that has been tightened recently.

The domestic market has been regulated by the so-called 'New Issues Committee', which was established in the late 1960s by the Swiss Bankers' Association, and in which practically the whole Swiss banking community is represented. Until recently this committee worked on a voluntary basis, although it was presided over by a senior member of the management of the Swiss National Bank.

Within the anti-inflation package adopted last year by the Swiss parliament, the New Issues Committee has been given official status: the Swiss government has appointed politicians as well as representatives of the Federal, Cantonal and Communal authorities to become members of this committee, which had formerly been composed exclusively of bankers. While the old New Issues Committee merely had the task of regulating the smooth functioning of the Swiss capital market, the new committee with a larger group of members is a tool of overall Swiss economic policy.

The committee's task is to regulate the new issue market with respect to bond and share offerings by domestic entities. Before the end of each quarter, the members of the committee meet in order to establish the programme and the total amount of new issues to be offered publicly during the following quarter. The amount made available for a given period depends on the needs of the borrowers, of course, and on the general state of the market, the purpose being to avoid congestion and excessive fluctuations of domestic interest rates.

However, it happens from time to time that the market

experiences such short-term fluctuations that the amount of new issues agreed upon initially can be increased or, conversely, must be reduced in the course of a quarter. Thus, some flexibility can be achieved within a relatively narrow market subject to controls.

This relative narrowness, and one has to emphasize the word relative, could be an obstacle to the financing of huge Swiss investment programmes abroad. Here again, however, our large industrial groups pursue a policy of self-financing to the largest extent possible. Nevertheless, there have been exceptions, for the approach taken in financing investments abroad is obviously not the same for all industries. Some prefer to finance their new venture programme with the parent company's or the consolidated cash flow, others stick to direct lending by the Swiss parent company, and some take up credits in the country where they are already established or will be investing.

There are also some large industrial concerns in a position to avail themselves of foreign capital markets or even with access to the Euromarket. The most relevant example in this respect is the Swiss aluminium industry, with its leader, Swiss Aluminium Ltd. This company has tapped several domestic and international capital markets via its affiliates in Australia, Iceland, Norway, the Netherlands, Antilles and the United Kingdom. Another Swiss company, CIBA-GEIGY Ltd., has borrowed publicly on the British market and privately on the French market; the former CIBA Corporation also borrowed publicly in the U.S. Both Swiss Aluminium Ltd. and CIBA-GEIGY came to the market with straight and equity-linked issues.

This chapter would be incomplete without reference to London as the centre of an international bond market, and in many ways a turn-table for capital, just as Switzerland has been —although inevitably on a smaller scale—during the post-war years. The unstable position of the pound on the foreign exchange markets, and more importantly the perpetuation of control over capital movements by the Bank of England as agent for the Treasury, have diverted overseas borrowing to other currencies. Thus London has come to play a leading role in euro-bond issues of various kinds, particularly those in euro-dollars, and there is an impressive array of euro-bond quotations to be found in the London Stock Exchange list. Where issues are made in currencies other than dollars (DM., fl., etc.), London still remains heavily involved, though only in a subordinate role. It is estimated that euro-bond issues during 1972 exceeded the equivalent of £2,000 million.

About half of the euro-bond issues are taken up by Swiss banks and placed predominantly in portfolios of their clients. While the yield on these bonds is usually very attractive, the fact that there is only a narrow secondary market once the bonds are sold presents certain dangers as regards the price development, which is usually subject to heavy fluctuations.

At the end of June last year the Swiss government had to take measures to ward off the enormous flow of foreign capital into the country. One of the restrictions introduced at that time, and still in force, is that the taking up of all credits abroad by non-banking entities in excess of S.fr. 1 million is subject to special permission from the Swiss National Bank. These temporary measures apply both to short-term borrowing and to the floating of long-term loans and bond issues abroad.

Medium- and short-term financing within the credit markets

THE SWISS CREDIT SYSTEM

Both from a practical and historical point of view it is useful to divide Swiss banks into three groups:

—the large commercial banks
—the cantonal banks

—all the other banks (local banks, savings banks, medium-size and small banks).

The third group also includes all the foreign-owned or foreign-controlled banks, with total assets amounting to some 10% of those of all Swiss banks taken together.

Traditionally, the cantonal banks, local and savings banks devote the major part of their credit activity to the granting of mortgage credits, while the financing of industry and commerce, and international banking activities, are almost exclusively carried out by the large commercial banks.

Although in principle this division of activities is still in force today, there is a definite trend towards universal banking, especially among the large commercial banks and a few of the big cantonal banks.

The granting of short- and medium-term credits to industry and commerce remains the classic credit transaction of the large Swiss commercial banks. This covers above all the provision of working capital to industrial and commercial companies for short-term financing of purchases of goods, bridging the period between deliveries and the receipt of payments, and for payment of wages and general costs which will be covered by earnings after a short delay. Even if such a credit line is often used by the borrower over a period of many years, it is, from an economic point of view, a short-term credit, since the funds from the bank are employed for a succession of transactions. The arrangement thus becomes a revolving credit to strengthen the working capital of the company.

Technically, the bank opens a credit line in favour of the borrower to be used in the form of an overdraft up to the agreed limit on a flexible day-to-day basis, whereby the borrower does not have to pay debit interest for fixed balances, possibly involving large amounts of idle funds. This system, which originated in the United Kingdom, is based upon a close understanding and trust between banker and customer and provides ready funds as needed at a very competitive rate.

As far as the bank is concerned, the granting of overdraft facilities creates certain problems with regard to its liquidity management. Experience has shown that the average utilization of such overdrafts is about 60% of the total limits open to commercial clients. The unused amounts represent a factor of uncertainty which the bank has to reckon with.

Provided the borrower can prove that over the past his company has had sufficient liquidity and earning power, and that the desired credit limit is in sound proportion to the capital and reserves of the company, the credit limit will be opened on an uncovered basis. If these conditions are not fulfilled, for instance in the case of recently established companies, or if larger funds are needed for further expansion of plant and equipment, the bank will ask for collateral either in the form of personal guarantees or real values (i.e. mortgages). Another reason for a borrower to put up collateral for a loan may be to take advantage of the more favourable interest rate the banks allow for covered credits.

When deciding on the credit-worthiness of a potential borrower, the banks also take into consideration whether the credit serves an economically useful purpose. This is for instance the case if, in view of the present rapid technological progress, a company is forced to renew its industrial equipment at a faster rate than in the past or if a situation arises where it becomes essential to acquire major interests in other firms in order to keep pace with mounting competition, and where the necessary funds can no longer be found out of retained profits, i.e. through self-financing. I shall revert to the complex problems of depreciation and self-financing later on.

In recent years the granting of medium-term finance credits to foreign borrowers has become increasingly important. At present these credits amount to about 10% of the total short- and medium-term lending activity of my bank, the Swiss Bank Corporation. One of the reasons behind the great demand for such credits is the U.S. government's policy of reducing the balance of payments deficit by setting up restrictions on U.S. corporations wishing to export capital for the financing of their foreign subsidiaries. This is why a large number of European subsidiaries of first-class American corporations have made credit applications to the Swiss commercial banks.

The Swiss banks are quite willing to comply with these credit requests to the extent that they have corresponding medium-term deposits at their disposal.

In Switzerland finance credits are not opened in the form of overdraft facilities, but rather as fixed loans with a prearranged currency period of one to five years, in exceptional cases up to seven years. The interest rates payable on these finance credits are usually fixed for the full duration of the loan on the basis of the rates the banks have to pay on their medium-term bank bonds (bons de caisse).

These medium-term bonds are a typically Swiss instrument which the banks have introduced to raise longer-term funds. The bonds are issued at par at interest rates varying according to the duration, which ranges from 3 to 8 years. They are sold to clients on a continuous basis, and thus have the big advantage for the banks that their due-dates are spread evenly and do not create a liquidity problem like large bond issues placed on the capital market. The medium-term bonds are not marketable, and therefore do not change in price during their currency period. They are not redeemable before due-date, unless the holder can claim exceptional circumstances and the bank is willing to accept them. However, medium-term bonds can be used as collateral if the holder needs a temporary bank credit. A large portion of these bonds are regularly renewed at their due-dates, as they represent a safe instrument of deposit with attractive interest rates. At the end of 1971 the total amount of such bonds outstanding at all banks in Switzerland amounted to S.fr. 25,000 million.

A very special and surprising feature of the Swiss credit system is the high level of mortgage debts of private owners of houses and land, and also of a great number of commercial and industrial firms. At the end of 1971 the total mortgage loans outstanding at all the Swiss banks amounted to S.fr. 46,000 million. One must add to this the mortgage credits granted by insurance companies, pension funds, finance companies etc., of an estimated total of some S.fr. 20–30,000 million. Most of these mortgage loans are legally callable at six months' notice but, as this provision is never exercised provided the interest is paid promptly, they are considered long-term borrowings.

FINANCING IN THE EURO-MARKETS

In the recent past the enormous size of the euro-market has been referred to by almost every economist trying to explain the massive movements of dollars into so-called strong European currencies. This is not the place to add yet another comment on the currency situation. From the point of view of source of funds for industry and commerce the euro-market plays a very important role. No doubt the ability of the banks to apply innovative methods of financing to satisfy the needs of multinational corporations has been demonstrated most conclusively in the euro-currency markets. The rapid expansion of so-called roll-over credits is but one example of the efficiency of this market. Obviously the old rule that a bank which borrows short and invests long must go bankrupt does not apply to the euro-currency transactions, at least as long as such transactions continue to be passed through a limited number of first-class banks.

I should like to add here a few remarks on the policy of Swiss banks as regards these roll-over credits. As you know, they are medium-term credits with maturities of up to five years, financed with short-term funds taken up in the euro-market. The interest rate on roll-over credits is fixed every six months—in accordance with the term of the deposits—on the basis of the interbank rate in London on the respective due-dates.

In view of the fact that, in the case of roll-over credits, medium-term commitments of the lender bank are financed with short-term funds, and also because such credits have often been used by the borrowers for the financing of their long-term investments and not only within the framework of their cash management, Swiss banks have in the past refused to grant such credits. However, developments on the international markets have shown that this new kind of credit instrument will presumably remain part of the international credit activities of banks, as it fulfils the needs of multinational corporations and their cash management. This is why the large Swiss commercial banks decided some time ago to participate in these roll-over credits. However, in order not to influence the internal interest rate structure in Switzerland, such credits are granted only in foreign currencies, mainly in U.S. dollars. Furthermore, the borrowers have to be corporations domiciled abroad, including foreign affiliates of Swiss corporations. By keeping to these restrictions the Swiss commercial banks hope to ward off any serious repercussions of euro-market borrowings on the Swiss credit market, which forms the backbone for the existence of all Swiss banks operating in the main locally—the cantonal and local banks. This is why the heavy fluctuations of interest rates on the euro-market must be prevented at all costs from influencing the interest rate structure in Switzerland.

In order to emphasize this division between the Swiss and the international money and capital markets, roll-over credits are usually granted through the intermediary of foreign affiliates of the large Swiss commercial banks.

The credit agreement usually contains a multi-currency clause whereby the debtor has the option of changing, at any due-date, the currency in which his debt is denominated into another one acceptable to the banks.

The centre for revolving credits financed on a roll-over basis by means of euro-currency deposits is in London, and American banks play a dominant role.

There seems little doubt that the future will bring about an increase in the volume of roll-over credits. Their maturities have already stretched, exceptionally, to ten years, thus entering the field of long-term finance normally made in the form of bond issues. The obvious consequence of this development will be that the banks operating in this market will have to make a very careful and detailed analysis of the credit-worthiness of potential borrowers. In fact it will be necessary to apply practices similar to those now customary when selecting corporations intending to issue bonds on any national or international market. This is the only way to prevent failures on the part of debtors, which could lead to catastrophic chain reactions and cause irreparable damage to the entire euro-market.

In order to minimize the risk of bad debts, euro-currency financing necessarily favours the well-known corporation with first-rate standing, obviating the need for checking even when large amounts are involved. Loans on the euro-market are made quickly with a minimum of red tape and little or no inquiry as to the purpose of the loan. It seems that each of the banks operating on the market relies implicitly on the judgement of the lending bank initiating the transaction. This puts a great responsibility on these banks.

While the well-known multinational corporations have no difficulty in raising funds on the euro-currency markets, the situation is entirely different for growing multinational firms whose standing and name have not yet been established for borrowing purposes. The euro-market is not designed to meet the need of today's smaller but rapidly expanding company, because it is a market where loans are made strictly on the standing of the borrower. Capacity to demonstrate ability to repay, either through current cash flow or the degree of success the company is likely to achieve if it receives additional funds, is only a determining factor in exceptional cases.

NOTE ISSUES IN SWISS FRANCS

In accordance with article 8 of the Swiss Banking Law, capital exports out of Switzerland with a maturity of 12 months or longer and an amount of S.fr. 10 million or more have to be submitted to the Swiss National Bank for approval. Thus the latter has the possibility of exercising effective control over foreign credits, the issue of foreign bonds in Switzerland, and the placement of medium-term notes.

While for foreign bond issues there is usually a fairly long waiting list of potential borrowers, the placement of medium-term notes can be arranged within a few weeks, depending on Swiss National Bank approval.

At present the following main conditions have to be fulfilled for the issue of such notes:

—the notes must be privately placed; a public issue with subsequent listing on the Swiss Stock Exchange is not possible; therefore, no prospectus is required and no publicity is allowed;

—the minimum denomination is S.fr. 20,000 for notes placed with Swiss residents and Swiss francs 50,000 for notes placed with non-residents;

—the notes must remain deposited with the bank applying for Swiss National Bank approval;

—65% of the notes must be placed with Swiss residents;

—the proceeds of notes issued have to be converted in Switzerland, according to their value on the payment date, into such foreign currency as the borrower may designate, at market conditions.

The notes usually have a maturity of five years. As a rule they are not syndicated, but underwritten and sold by one individual commercial bank alone. The interest rates paid on these notes are about $\frac{1}{4}$% above the rates paid on foreign bond issues placed in Switzerland. However, as the notes are not publicly issued, but placed privately, the costs and commissions charged by the banks to the borrowers are smaller.

In 1971 medium-term notes totalling S.fr. 5,000 million were issued in Switzerland; in 1972 the respective figure was slightly lower. These amounts compare with total foreign bond issues of S.fr. 2,000 million in 1971 and S.fr. 2,900 million in 1972.

MULTINATIONAL BANKING IN RELATION TO FINANCING OF INDUSTRY, COMMERCE, AND MULTINATIONAL CORPORATIONS

In order to be able to keep up with the rapidly expanding multinational corporations, the large commercial banks operating predominantly in the international field have had to extend the range of services they provide for this most important class of clients. First of all, the credit amounts required by multinationals are now much larger than used to be the case some years ago. Medium-term loans up to ten or twelve years amounting to $100 million are no longer unusual. As examples, I should like to mention the loan of $250 million taken up by Philips Lamps in 1970, and the financing of British Petroleum last year which amounted to the staggering total of £360 million.

Furthermore, international banks must be prepared, if national regulations permit, to arrange for credit facilities for their customers which can be utilized in various countries and in various currencies—so-called multicurrency loans—again on a scale previously unheard of.

Another service the multinationals require from their bankers is that of so-called international cash management, which includes optimizing the collection of corporate receipts and disbursement of payments, and locating multicurrency clearing, usually in one centre that can net out the corporations' transactions in many countries and many currencies.

How have the banks reacted to this new challenge?

Some large American banks have followed the multinational corporations in establishing a world-wide network of subsidiaries. Other U.S. banks have concentrated their international activities in a few selected financial centres such as London and opened their own subsidiaries there.

The European banks have either formed ad hoc syndicate arrangements to carry out specific operations or entered into liaisons on a permanent basis. Examples of the latter are the many multinational medium-term banks, chiefly established in London.

Other European banks have joined with American banks to form multinational banking groups. The members of some of these are themselves leading banks in their own countries, so that the respective combines are very powerful entities. Since it is likely that the trend towards the formation of such groups will continue, I should like to mention here four of the most interesting:

The first is the European Banks' International Company (E.B.I.C.), the oldest of the four. Membership is made up of one large commercial bank each in Holland, Germany, England, Belgium, France and Austria. Then there is the CCB-Group consisting of the Commerzbank in Germany, the French Crédit Lyonnais and the Banco di Roma in Italy. The third group, the Société Financière Européenne (S.F.E.), is made up of a bank in each of the following countries: Holland, Italy, France, Belgium, England, Germany, Japan and the United States. Finally, there are the banking institutions established under the name of Orion, whose membership consists of an American, a British, a Canadian, a German, an Italian and a Japanese bank.

So far, the three leading Swiss banks, which do a significant amount of international business, have not joined any of these groups. There are a number of reasons for this attitude. First of all, the Swiss banks have never met with any difficulties in putting together ad hoc syndicates whenever this became necessary. Furthermore, they feel that many of their clients are very much attracted by the fact that the large Swiss banks are completely independent and have managed to maintain their national character. Another point is that the development of the multinational banking groups has not yet shown clearly whether the advantages outweigh the disadvantages. Finally, the three leading Swiss commercial banks have widened their network of subsidiaries abroad (London, New York, Tokyo, etc.) and have also increased the number of representatives all over the world.

This does not mean that the attitude taken so far by the Swiss banks is inflexible. We live in a rapidly changing world, and it has always been the policy of Swiss banks to adapt their activities to new developments.

LEASING AND FACTORING

Owing to the limited financial resources of many companies faced with the need to keep up with latest technical developments in order to remain competitive, it is becoming more and more difficult to find the required long-term financing for investment in fixed assets. Therefore, many assets such as office and store buildings, all kinds of equipment from special machines to office computers, and even cars, delivery trucks etc., are no longer bought outright, but rented. Newly-established firms with only limited capital rely particularly on leasing facilities, as their capital is tied up to a large extent in the financing of inventories and accounts receivable.

The commercial banks are both willing and well-equipped to finance current assets of commercial and industrial corporations, whereby the credit amounts made available by the banks are continuously repaid out of sales proceeds. I have already mentioned the various credit forms and possibilities at the disposal of large and small commercial clients.

Normally fixed assets—plant and equipment—should be financed from a company's own resources. Provided a corporation is sufficiently large and well-known, it also has the possibility of raising long-term funds on the capital market. But not many corporations have sufficient funds to cover their long-term investments through self-financing, or are sufficiently large to launch bonds on the capital market. This is where leasing comes in. Thus, in 1964, the Swiss Bank Corporation established a fully-owned leasing company, which has since become the leader in its field in Switzerland. Between 1969 and 1972 the turnover of the leasing company went up by more than 500%. The largest portion of the business is the leasing of capital goods, office machines, computers, machine tools, plant and equipment. It is interesting to note that not only small companies apply for leasing facilities. In fact the largest group of clients of our bank's leasing company are shareholding companies with a capital between S.fr. 1 and 5 million.

I am convinced that the future will see a further development of leasing arrangements, since these enable the client to calculate the exact costs and save him from having to find long-term capital in order to keep up with his investment needs.

In the United States many companies are taking advantage of another financing procedure known as 'sale and leaseback', where business firms already owning land and buildings sell them to large institutional investors such as insurance companies or pension funds on the understanding that the property will be leased back for a period of years. Such procedures are especially popular with large department store chains.

Another service banks offer through special subsidiaries is factoring. Many industrial and commercial companies are burdened by having to carry large volumes of accounts receivable. In these cases the factoring company assumes responsibility for the collection of accounts both in Switzerland and abroad. The client can also pass on to the factoring company the risk of bad debts and the ledgering of receivables. Furthermore, the factoring company is willing to advance receivables before maturities. In this case the client has to pledge his accounts as security for the loan.

The rate of interest charged by the factoring company on advances of receivables corresponds to the current rate charged by banks on overdrafts. In addition, the client has to pay a fee of between slightly less than 1% and up to about 2% of the turnover. This fee varies in accordance with the size of the turnover, i.e. the number of sales per year, the number of accounts, the quality of the debts and whether or not the risk of bad debts is assumed by the factoring company. As a general rule it can be said that the smaller the turnover and the average amount of the accounts receivable, the higher the factoring fee. A large number of small accounts cause more work and are therefore more costly.

Experience both in Switzerland and abroad shows that, from an annual turnover of S.fr. 1 million upwards, factoring can become advantageous for both the client and the factoring company. From the point of view of the factoring company there is no upper limit, provided refinancing can be arranged.

Self-financing as the cardinal Swiss principle

As a result of the limited size of the Swiss market, the large Swiss corporations were forced very early to rely heavily on the development of exports if they wanted to continue their expansion. Parallel to this they opened their own production companies abroad. Thus corporations such as Brown Boveri, CIBA-GEIGY, Hoffmann-La Roche, Nestlé, Sandoz, and Sulzer can be considered to be some of the first multinational concerns. There are in fact only a few companies outside Switzerland which have such a high percentage of exports, and at the same time produce such large portions of their total output outside the home country.

Multinational operations carry a very high degree of risk, which makes these corporations follow a conservative finance policy. The difficulties encountered by these corporations during the thirties, when they were forced to rely heavily on borrowed funds, induced them to return to the system of self-financing after the last war when they entered a new phase of expansion. However, while in the pioneering days of industrial development self-financing was conducted with earnings belonging to the owners of the company, the funds now used belong to a large number of shareholders.

Traditionally the development of the large Swiss industrial corporations is based on research-intensive products or goods requiring a high amount of skill and precision work. In these sectors the optimum size of a corporation, able to compete internationally, is fairly large. This in turn means that the history of Swiss industry is characterized by high research expenditure, heavy capital investment, the availability of skilled labour and the necessity for mergers.

The high portion of research expenditure in the total production costs of large Swiss corporations causes difficult problems of finance. The risk factor of research costs is particularly high in view of the uncertainty of the marketability of a new product, its quality in comparison to new developments of competitors, and the open question as to whether the new product will qualify for patent protection. For all these reasons research expenditure must be covered by long-term financing, preferably by internal resources of the corporations concerned, as the actual results and earnings are too uncertain and too far in the future. The large Swiss corporations are well aware of this fact, and finance their research projects entirely from within without having recourse to the capital market.

Owing to the rapid rate of technical progress, a major portion of the output of Swiss industry is relatively short-lived as regards its position on world markets. It is therefore difficult for the corporations concerned to place a value on their equipment and machinery. Its actual value may vary considerably according to the success of research efforts. This is another reason why research costs must be financed out of current earnings. The resulting growth fully justifies this procedure, which is also in the long-term interest of the shareholders.

The situation is, of course, different if a corporation plans to expand its capacities for the output of well-established products which are likely to retain their good market position in the foreseeable future. The financing of such expansions could be raised in the capital market or in the form of long-term loans. But even in these cases most large Swiss corporations prefer to rely on their capacity for self-financing, in view of the fairly high risks of their multinational activities.

SELF-FINANCING AND DEPRECIATION PROCEDURES

More and more frequently the term 'cash flow' appears in annual reports of Swiss corporations and in press releases. The term itself is misleading, as neither the profit nor the depreciation included in the cash flow represents an actual input of funds. They can be part of any asset of the corporation concerned such as goods, receivables, participations, etc., and usually only a small amount consists of liquid funds. Depreciation, which represents the dominant part of the cash flow, consists of costs allotted to individual products for the necessary renewal of machinery and equipment, and also partly covers risks on products that might not be sold, on doubtful receivables, etc. Depreciation as a percentage of total costs varies with the current competitive and price situation of the corporation.

The actual amounts written off are constantly used for the updating of equipment and machinery, the financing of inventories and outstanding receivables. In the widest sense depreciation funds are also applied for the financing of research expenditure, at least that part of research necessary to keep the technology of the corporation up-to-date. This shows that it is difficult to make a clear distinction between depreciation and retained profits. Part of the depreciation is reserved for the replacement, renewal and improvement of fixed assets, while the actual self-financing out of retained profits only occurs if the earnings of a company are big enough to cover part or all of the financing of enlargements of available capacities.

NEW TRENDS IN SWISS COMPANY LAW

Proposals are now being prepared for the partial revision of Swiss Company Law. The present situation is that, in accordance with the Swiss Federal Code of Obligations, the board and management of a corporation are entitled to create so-called 'hidden reserves'. These reserves do not appear in the balance sheet or in the profit and loss statement. They consist of depreciation and profits on any asset of the corporation, with no equivalent amount on the liabilities side of the balance sheet, contrary to the open reserves.

The main purpose of hidden reserves is to make it possible for the administration to stabilize published annual profits and dividends paid. In other words, in good years, the company shows profits that are too low and in bad years some of the hidden reserves are reactivated to increase profits.

One of the proposals made by the working group preparing the revision of the Swiss Company Law is that these hidden reserves, together with the necessary depreciation, are to be shown in the profit and loss statement, but not in the balance sheet. An estimate of the actual reserves—the so-called hidden reserves—would have to be mentioned in the annual report. In order to counteract the present high rate of inflation in Switzerland, the Federal authorities have, among other measures, decided to limit the maximum depreciation rates as a temporary means of increasing tax revenues and thus reducing the money supply in circulation.

Methods of financial planning

The task of financial planning as part of overall corporate planning is to ascertain that the funds necessary for future investments can be obtained as cheaply as possible, provided this does not jeopardize the survival of the corporation.

The costs a corporation has to pay for its funds depend on two factors:

—the costs of individual elements of the capital structure;

—the composition of these individual elements or, in other words, the capital structure as such.

While it is easy to assess the costs of funds from outside sources, this is not so in the case of the costs of internal resources, and in particular those of retained profits and other items included in the term cash flow. The system most frequently applied in this connection is the concept of the so-called 'opportunity cost', i.e. what yield would be expected if these funds were invested outside the corporation concerned. This yield is composed of the following elements:

—the yield on risk-free long-term investments

—the general corporate risk (risk on assets)

—the specific risk resulting from the general financial position of the corporation (risk of liabilities).

This means that the costs of the internal resources of a corporation depend on its earning power. High earning power lowers the capital costs and vice versa. The importance of the financial position as regards the costs of the internal capital of a corporation determines the importance of an overall sound balance sheet structure, which not only lowers the costs of the internal capital but also those of the funds from outside.

Another factor is that a high leverage up to the limit acceptable by the market also contributes to a lowering of the costs of the internal capital of a corporation.

Thus there is—at least theoretically—an optimal financial structure for each corporation, and it is the task of sound financial planning to find a financial structure that is as close as possible to this optimum.

In reality, however, the planning concept of a corporation is not based purely on financial considerations. A corporation may be willing to accept certain financial sacrifices in order to pursue other aims, as for instance independence from capital markets.

A survey made last year among eleven large Swiss corporations revealed clearly that, while all their investment decisions are made on the basis of yield calculations, their financial policy is only motivated partly—if at all—by the effort to limit their capital costs. Three of the eight corporations replying to the questions submitted to them admitted that they do not apply the concept of capital costs. As regards using the leverage factor, the survey showed that four of the corporations either have no outside funds at all or have raised some funds from outside sources, but in more or less arbitrary fashion, without considering the limits the market would set for their debt capacity. All the corporations declared that their dividend policy is not influenced by favourable investment possibilities.

The results of this survey show the importance of aims other than purely financial ones. These aims are for instance the long term consolidation of the market position of the corporation, the furthering of its image, or—very important—maintaining its independence. Most of the corporations stated that their overall strategy is to keep a balance between the various pressure groups (shareholders, suppliers, clients, etc.). The higher the degree of self-financing a corporation is able to pursue, the greater its independence. This in turn means higher costs for the total working capital.

One point emerges quite clearly from replies to the survey: under today's conditions, with rapid political, technological and monetary changes, financing decisions have far-reaching effects and must be taken on the basis of concrete financial planning. This is why the large Swiss commercial banks have established special departments for the assistance of industrial and commercial clients in questions of overall corporate policy. This includes not only financial planning, but also assistance in mergers and acquisitions, in finding new foreign markets, in discussing the possibilities of using higher leverage, and in finding the optimum size in order to be able to cope with rapidly changing environments.

Advice for Industry and Commerce

by C. H. Villiers, M.C.

'Mind your own business' is a good precept in affairs as well as in life. We all resent uninvited comments on our behaviour, in our business and on how we conduct our affairs. The candid friend can soon find he has few friends left, even helpful hints by jolly old uncles are usually resented. And yet . . . there must be something wrong with this diagnosis because the consultants have never been busier, the psychoanalysts' couches are practically hot beds, and for the confessionals in church queues are forming.

Perhaps the fact is that we do really all know that we need help and advice in our doings, but we want it from professionals and not from friends or amateurs. We want it clinical, we want it experienced and we want it private. If need be we will pay for it, but we want to feel free to reject it, usually we believe what we want to hear, but also we generally do what we are forcefully pressurized to do. So the role of the adviser is difficult, it is dicey and it can be dangerous to valuable relationships.

It is perhaps for these reasons that bankers in the U.K. at all events have been particularly hesitant about giving advice to their customers. It was certainly not always so—the private banker took a special pride in the success of his customers and in his influence over them. Today the machinery of banking is so vast and intruding that the humanities (if that is the right word) of banking tend to become obscured. In any event a bank manager, struggling for promotion, hesitates long before giving advice which, if wrong, might lose the bank a customer—the manager's worst sin. I once asked the chairman of a very big bank if he would rather lose money or lose a customer. 'A good question,' quoth he, 'depending on the customer!'

So there are bankers who not only refuse to advise customers except on non-controversial technical matters, but would advise other bankers to avoid the counselling process as being outside the banking business. A banker is a financial intermediary, they claim, and he must look after his own business and not after other people's problems. 'Am I my brother's keeper?' is a question as old as the world itself. There is nothing pejorative in this attitude: it is cautious, conservative, traditional, and it is certainly appropriate for those bankers who, perhaps for good reasons, prefer not to lift their eyes to the wider horizons of business.

STRATEGICAL PROBLEMS

But I cannot accept that you who come to the Summer School are necessarily bankers of that mould. It must surely be that you have been selected to come here because of your promise, your potential, your possibility of rising to the higher echelons of your banks where the strategical problems of business are considered every day. Indeed this may be the important distinction to make here: if you wish to limit your view to tactics, keep to giving technical advice. If however it is the strategy of business which attracts you, you must broaden out your knowledge and experience to the big problems which from time to time come up in front of all business men. They and you may turn aside from them, but don't forget that a tactical solution to a strategical problem only postpones it, and it will surely recur in a more difficult form.

I hope you will forgive my spending some time on this aspect of advice to customers, but I want you to think deeply about it.

Especially important is it just now when the business environment is changing so violently and so fast. I remember twenty years ago when a take-over was a rare and dramatic event. I recall my then chairman, Lionel Fraser, ringing up the chairman of a great industrial company on behalf of one of our clients and saying in awesome tones 'I have a communication of great importance to put to you at your earliest convenience'. Later he and Siegmund Warburg won the great battle for British Aluminium for Tube Investments and Reynolds, and it was he who persuaded Charles Clore not to press home his bid for Watneys. But in those days change was slow and wrongly resisted. Today it races ahead and has, indeed, in some areas got ahead of itself. Technology, stimulated by the war and harnessed to peaceful uses, is probably at the root of it. Inflation has stoked it up. Big buying power by young people and organized workers has helped it along. Entry into E.E.C. is about to add a new dimension to business change, for which we are hardly ready. New laws, new taxes, new controls form new parameters within which new men find new opportunities, new markets and create new fashions. All this provides a wonderful liberation of energies and imagination. The banks in their own business have seen much of it—freedom to compete, freedom to lend, freedom to invest, freedom to merge, but it is in the very exercise of these freedoms that bankers have a greater power, a larger responsibility towards their customers, which is more far-reaching, more important, more intimate in a way than ever before. It is this series of relationships that I should now like to discuss with you.

VICTIMS OF CHANGE

In the summary of this talk I find I have listed questions of a defensive nature—the questions of the stranded fish, the extinct volcanoes, the victims of change. They are, of course, important, and they need more help. But the thrusters, the go-getters, have their problems too, and will probably never get off the launching pad without a banker's help. So we must also look at what advice to give to them.

But let us now look at a customer in a declining or overcrowded industry. In a mature, indeed old economy, such as ours, these cases are frequent, they are difficult, sometimes painful. Some would say they should go out of business and let others, more modern and more vigorous, get hold of their properties and assets and manpower and put them to better use. This was the philosophy which led the present U.K. government to adopt its initial policy towards what it called lame ducks. It was not a success. It led to highly damaging collapses in which everybody lost (not least the banks) and ultimately to asset stripping, which brings the whole financial system into total disrepute.

I have seen an enormous amount of this problem during nearly thirty years as a merchant banker, including three years as Managing Director of the Industrial Reorganization Corporation, and I am sure that good bankers can greatly help themselves, their customers and the economy by early, firm and experienced advice. Declining companies are usually 'in the bank' and the banker's leverage is considerable. He has the right, indeed the duty, to enquire as to how his money is being used, and this provides the opportunity for the giving of what I have called clinical, experienced and private advice.

There are four things a company in a declining or overcrowded industry can do. First, it can 'trade up'. It is likely that the decline and overcrowding is taking place at the cheaper, traditional end of the market. As people, the consumers, have got richer, so have their desires for something better, more sophisticated, just different. The U.K. machine tool industry, for example, bangs on with traditional machines, allowing others to pinch our markets with newer, more versatile types. The village grocer is overtaken by the better marketing of the supermarkets and the cash and carry shops. The local brewer finds life almost impossible in competition with the big national brewers. But let them 'trade up', and at once they have a chance of survival.

Secondly, they can merge. This is often right: it means finding a compatible partner, it means surrendering some sovereignty, some independence. The arguments for merging are so well known as to be boring, but it is the answer to the problems of many companies in declining industries.

Thirdly, your customer can set out on the takeover trail if he is energetic, or sell out if he is passive.

Fourthly, there can be a change of management. We shall think more about this later on, but there are today two key men in any company, the managing director and the financial director. Many companies simply don't have any one at board level looking after the finances: a book-keeper won't do. If these two key appointments are wrong the company won't survive, and the banker may lose his money.

Somewhere among these four courses of action lies a mix that will get the company out of its decline. The trouble is that each of these four courses is difficult, unpopular, and is naturally avoided. The tendency is to put off decision, to sweep the problem under the carpet, to hope it will go away. It is here that the banker's advisory role is crucial and effective. The banker will probably not know the circumstances so well that he can prescribe exact action, but he can push and prod for sensible action to be taken in good time, and he can use his money power to make it happen. All of you here now will have, if you have not already experienced, an opportunity to help a customer in this situation. If you feel you can't cope, belt up or send for a bigger gun. But if you feel you *can* help, use your commonsense, put yourself in the customer's shoes, and use your money power discreetly to nudge him irresistibly towards the decision which he probably knows in the end he will be forced to take. But it is so much better to do it in good time—before it is too late.

It fell to Geoffrey Robinson (now Managing Director of

Innocenti) and myself in 1969 at the Industrial Reorganization Corporation to do all this for the mining machinery industry, which was in serious decline and very overcrowded. We used all the techniques I have just mentioned. We brought it down from 12 to four companies, which are now all good, strong, well-managed exporting concerns. If the industry had collapsed, the shareholders, managers, the labour, the banks and the economy would have suffered. I submit that much of that work could, indeed should, have been done by the banks which, instead, sat in a dazed way, slightly negative, watching it all happen.

DIVERSIFICATION

The second situation I have listed is how to broaden the base of a company. This must be handled with especial care. There is a great tendency to wish to diversify in industry and commerce today, and this has much merit if handled correctly; but if it is done wrongly it is disastrous. The principle is quite clear: if a company has as its basic discipline mechanical engineering, or contracting, or being a financial intermediary or selling to individual consumers, then it is very unwise in its diversification programme to venture out of that discipline into fields which its management will find unfamiliar and foreign to the existing ethos of the company. Very many serious company collapses have come this way, and the banker should be very alert to the possibilities of disaster through diversification. The banker will certainly be consulted because of the need for finance, and I submit that it is the banker's role at that point not just to ask how the new diversification will be managed, but to press hard on how it fits within the existing management expertise of the customer's company. I have used this simile before, but look at your hands and see how the bone structure, tissues, blood vessels and nerves allow the ten fingers to be articulated and controlled by the same management centre—the brain. Try to graft on a nose or a toe or any other member and you will get rejection, because there is no natural affinity or control to make the graft work. It is very much like that in business: you can control about ten divisions with natural affinities, but if you get more or lack affinity you are in for trouble. Many diversifications under the name of broadening the base of the business have been disasters because they were unnatural, and were seized upon either as a means of buying cheap profits or of gratifying the power complexes of ambitious managements. If I may again quote a case from experience, I would ask you to look at Courtaulds, where I am a director. Courtaulds is an enormous group, but all the development is in textiles. There was a diversification into international paints, but now the whole thrust of a huge cash flow is into a multi-fibre vertical textile group operating in many countries. It is not easy to manage, but the discipline and the expertise is the same throughout, and management can be switched to cope with problems and opportunities. In my own group, Guinness Peat, we have a very broad base as bankers, merchants, brokers and industrial entrepreneurs, but we always act as financial intermediaries and do not attempt more than that.

TAKE-OVER ANXIETIES

Now once a banker has started to talk to his customer along these lines—which concern the strategical aspect of business—he will certainly find cropping up anxieties about whether a take-over may be coming from a competitor or rival. At this point the commercial banker, as opposed to the merchant banker, should remember that discretion is the better part of valour, and avoid getting involved in how to conduct an effective defence against an unwanted take-over. This is a highly specialized and technical subject; much more than common-sense is needed, and a leading merchant banking house should be brought in. It may well be that the customer knows a merchant banker already, or perhaps the commercial bank has an in-house merchant banking capability, but whatever happens the commercial banker should not get too deeply involved or he may burn his fingers and lose his customer.

Fourthly, we should now consider the renewal of management. I devoted my Lubbock Memorial lecture in Oxford in 1971 to this subject, and I was very gratified when the Governor of the Bank of England took up half of my thesis and has now got a shareholders' watchdog to chase dozey managements, and when the Confederation of British Industry appointed a committee under Lord Watkinson which took up the other half and recommended more influence for the non-executive director on boards. It is not easy: I have referred earlier to the importance of the managing director and the finance director. I have found these the key men: the chairman should not be managing director except in unusual and temporary circumstances. The production, marketing and personnel directors are most important, but their functions are better understood and they are more easily replaced than the managing director and the finance man.

The banker will have become alerted to bad management through his own sixth sense, or by the company's poor results, or by managements' failure to produce up-to-date financial results. If the banker asks to see management accounts which are not more than three months old, and these are not made available to him, he has cause to become suspicious. Either they are not being produced at all, or they are distasteful, and the management is covering up hoping for better times.

Let there be no doubt about it—all companies go through difficult times. Contracts go wrong, you get caught on the wrong foot in markets or foreign exchange or commodities. Political events change the environment for companies quite unexpectedly, especially where there is heavy dependence on government for contracts or orders. Nevertheless, if a company persistently falls down on its performance, the banker must begin to wonder if this is a concern in which he can risk his depositors' money. At this point my own recipe is to find someone in the company in a position of responsibility to whom one can talk with a view to backing him in any management change. The banker can only work from people within the company. If things get really bad, the banker can appoint new management as a *quid pro quo* for continued financial support, but obviously it is desirable to get things right before that becomes necessary. If there really is nobody to back in the company, the banker must start to think of withdrawing support and of getting his money back; losing the account if necessary.

USING MONEY POWER

Usually, however, there are one or two people at or near the top of a company, perhaps non-executive directors, who are alarmed at the way things are going, and who are glad to find in the banker a like-minded friend who will help them to get things right. From then on the banker must play it by ear, but he must not shirk from using the money power and from using it early rather than late. One day at the Industrial Reorganization Corporation a famous banker brought a famous company to see me, saying the company could not pay the wages next week and the bankers would lend no more. This was brinkmanship with a vengeance. We persuaded the bankers to continue their support for another month while we investigated, then we changed the whole board and much of the management, and put in a lot of subordinated capital. Today that group has millions on deposit in the bank, having repaid all loans, and the share price is seven times the level of those sad days. There are examples of bankers being very successful in this way: the trouble is that it is nearly always left too late. Changing boards and management should not be left till disaster has occurred. Bankers are or should be the first to be aware of trouble. They should, I believe, have a fire brigade of their own who could help local controls to cope with these management problems with more dispassionate authority than the bank branch manager can, in these circumstances, normally muster. When trouble is scented nobody wants to know, because nobody wants the odium of making changes. Accountants and consultants can be brought in to report; hopefully the new City watchdog for shareholders will be active and useful, but bankers carry a big responsibility. The existence of large hidden or inner reserves blunts the banker's judgment in these circumstances, and the spate of take-overs lets the banker think that in the end someone will bale him out by taking the company over. All this has commercial validity, but it is not the way we are going to get a renewal of our national health or restore our position in the big wide world, and I think it should be more widely discussed.

I see that in a rash moment some months ago I said I would talk about new capital and expansion overseas. These are pretty technical subjects, and I think it best just to say that a banker should be acquainted with the rudiments of these vital subjects, and know where to advise his customers to go for the best advice. We have splendid capital markets in the City of London, and it is a pity not to make use of them. By the same token we are undertaking more expansion into Europe, the Far East and Africa than any other nation except the Americans. Excellent advice is available from bankers specializing in those areas, but they are tricky subjects, and ill-advised companies will come a cropper.

THE IMPATIENT CUSTOMER

And so to the advice the banker should give to the expansionist, the entrepreneur, the go-go boys, the asset stripper, the energetic, rough, self-confident impatient customer. There was a time when these got short shrift from the traditional commercial bankers, who were frightened of them, and they went to near-banks and got all the money they wanted—and paid through the nose for it, too! I believe all these people are essential to the mixed economy in which we live. So much of our society is bound up with government—50% of all investment is now from public funds—that the other half must be especially entrepreneurial to keep the balance true. The danger is, of course, that they will over-extend themselves, that they will not prove to be as good as they think they are. This is where the banker's traditional judgment comes in. If I may be allowed a personal word, it is that, in 1939, when I was in Glyn Mills Bank, I got married, and the chairman came to my wedding and said he thought I might do quite well in the bank provided I remembered the simple rule: 'Find a good man and lend him money'! I commend this ancient rule of thumb when dealing with the whizz kids but, to be sure he is kept in bounds, don't lend without security.

Well, you have had a bit of an ear-bashing from me on this matter of advice a banker should give to his customer on strategical matters in what are often rather awkward circumstances. The thing is not to go beyond the limits of your competence or confidence—if in doubt belt up, or send for a bigger gun, because this is big game hunting. But, if you feel on firm ground, play your hand carefully and thoughtfully and helpfully to get your customer's confidence. He certainly has problems, he certainly needs a confidant, he certainly wants your money; if you can show you know your way around, that you are discreet, that you are professional, you will get more business for your bank, you will help the creation of wealth we so much need, and you will on the way get a good promotion for yourself.

International Trade Finance

by K. H. Beyen

The Background

The gradual disintegration of the Bretton Woods monetary system—its causes and its consequences—has during the past years been one of the main topics of discussion amongst economists and financial experts all over the world. The complexity of the problem, and the upheavals and disturbances which we have witnessed, may sometimes have led us to see things in the wrong perspective or to put too much emphasis on symptoms rather than on fundamental issues.

One such fundamental issue, and a most important one, is the financing of international trade, and the following remarks will attempt to find some answers to the problems created in this area. But first it will be necessary to outline, as briefly as possible, the historical background.

The monetary system which developed during the nineteenth century was based on the assumption that general economic equilibrium would be reached when price-levels were determined exclusively by the free and untrammelled forces of the market and the monetary system functioned in complete accordance with the rules of the gold standard. With respect to international economic relations, this classical approach meant that, in order to allow comparative costs to have their full impact, trade should be as free as possible, and that the gold standard, with its automatic system for adjusting imbalances, should be scrupulously applied.

As a consequence of the economic crisis of the twenties and thirties, however, the system had to be abandoned. It was replaced by policies which sought to attain such objectives as full employment, price stability and equilibrium in the balance of payments by non-automatic economic and monetary policies. These objectives were meant to cure the social and economic ills which western countries were suffering from as a result of the depression, but they mostly ignored the previous international monetary system and in many instances were forced to violate it. However, whereas the objectives themselves were, and still are, felt to be amongst the inescapable obligations of all responsible governments, the international consequences of their pursuit were by no means generally accepted. Here, as in so many other instances, there was a strong desire to have one's cake and eat it: on the one hand a socially responsible economic policy within each country, allowing for monetary and budgetary measures to carry out national objectives; on the other hand a system of free world trade allowing for the greatest possible opportunity for everyone to expand his exports.

THE BRETTON WOODS SYSTEM

It is the great and historic achievement of the founding fathers of Bretton Woods to have performed this tour de force and to have created a system which for almost a quarter of a century allowed the world to strive after these two not necessarily consistent objectives simultaneously.

From the old gold standard, the Bretton Woods system had adopted, of course, many elements, such as stable exchange rates with small fluctuating margins and a high degree of convertibility. The requirement of 'fundamental disequilibrium' as the only justification for changing parities gave considerable stability and confidence as long as 'the dollar was as good as gold', in other words as long as the foundations on which the system had been erected remained unquestioned in their stability and reliability.

During this period, by which I mean the first twenty-odd years after the end of the second world war, international monetary problems and the liberalization of international trade used to be thought of as two separate issues.

Monetary questions were discussed within the framework of Bretton Woods and of its possible adaptations, such as the widening of the band and the introduction of Special Drawing Rights. On the other hand, efforts to liberalize world trade were carried out in G.A.T.T. (General Agreement on Tariffs and Trade), U.N.C.T.A.D. (United Nations Trade and Development Conference) and on a regional basis in such organizations as E.E.C. and E.F.T.A.

Assuming that the liquidation of the Bretton Woods system began on 15 August, 1971, one could take that date also as the beginning of the end—at least theoretically—of the separation between these two issues. In that context, the period 15 August–18 December, 1971 would have to be regarded as an interim period which was terminated by the Smithsonian Agreement.

THE SMITHSONIAN AGREEMENT

This agreement was arrived at in the expectation of a definite reform of the world monetary system. Initially, it was thought that the world would have to work in accordance with the agreement whilst in the meantime a new and definite concept would be prepared which at a certain date would become operative.

In fact, however, things went quite differently. On the one hand, the Smithsonian Agreement proved to be insufficiently solid to hold out between 18 December 1971 and the moment at which the new system could be introduced, and on the other hand the drawing up of a new monetary system appears to be much more difficult and complicated than was expected.

The present situation

A comprehensive new plan will not be available in the near future. As a consequence, we probably cannot expect more than the return of a limited amount of stability during a fairly long interim period without any definite new monetary system in sight.

In these circumstances we have to ask ourselves the following questions:

(*a*) What will be the consequences of a prolonged situation of floating exchange rates—at least between the dollar and the many other currencies? Assuming that international trade requires stable international monetary conditions for its optimum functioning, to what extent can it still function in a satisfactory manner under conditions of monetary instability? In other words, can international trade flourish without stable exchange rates?

(*b*) How can international trade be protected against damaging consequences resulting from this situation and what can the banks do to assist them?

FLEXIBLE EXCHANGE RATES

With respect to the first question, I feel that much of this is a matter of degree. There can be no doubt that strong fluctuations and considerable instability create great problems for international trade.

A 1971 inquiry by 'The Conference Board' into the experience of flexible rates of exchange produced the following result: 'a sizeable group of respondents reported a host of problems created by the float, such as greater caution displayed by customers, reluctance on the part of buyers to be billed in dollars, deals that were postponed, and an increased complexity of doing business in general.'

It would appear from this conclusion, drawn from statements by major trading companies, that the main problem they are faced with under present circumstances is lack of confidence. It is this basic feeling of insecurity on the part of those participating in international trade that either frustrates certain transactions or makes them more costly and more complicated to carry out. Let me give you an example.

A Scandinavian shipowner orders a ship to be built by a yard in Germany. The ship will subsequently be chartered to an American oil company. Payment for the ship will be effected in German marks but the charter under which it will be operated will be expressed in dollars.

The shipowner will finance the operation by contracting a medium-term euro-currency loan on a roll-over basis. A few years ago, this would have been a perfectly simple operation. The income from the charter being in U.S. dollars, the loan would have to be also in dollars to exclude foreign exchange exposure. Each time an instalment had to be paid to the shipyard, the shipowner would take up part of the loan and change it into D.M. to make the payment.

The subsequent threats of D.M. revaluation, however, forced the shipowner to seek additional protective measures such as paying for the ship in advance or purchasing D.M. bonds with the entire proceeds of the dollar loan and selling them as the payment for the ship became due, this latter method being chosen to forego the loss of interest resulting from a straight pre-payment. Such an operation, however, is costly in any event, and unusually complicated because of German regulations against the influx of funds from abroad.

Without going into all the technical details, it is clear that increasing uncertainty about the movements of foreign exchange rates are a material impediment to international transactions, particularly if they are stretched out over a period of several years. For shorter periods, say up to one year, the major trading currencies can still be bought or sold forward. Provided the forward exchange market functions well, there is no problem except that in a period of monetary upheavals far more transactions are covered forward than is otherwise the case, making them that much more expensive.

'LEADS AND LAGS'

The example I mentioned is, of course, a typical case of 'leads and lags', which have become a factor of the first magnitude in the present monetary situation. All those engaged in international trade, and all treasurers of international corporations, are more or less forced to apply it, and the effects are probably much greater than all the speculative movements by individuals in the euro-currency markets put together. In fact, it is not at all easy to draw a precise line between leads and lags on the one hand and foreign exchange speculation on the other: it all depends on what you call speculation. Every responsible merchant or treasurer will pay his obligations in strong currencies as quickly as possible and postpone his obligations in weak currencies as long as he can, provided that the interest costs this may entail are less than the foreign exchange loss or profit he expects to avoid or obtain by leading or lagging.

But this practice belongs in the category of self-fulfilling prophecies, as we have witnessed during these past years. In Italy, where exports have been performing quite well, the leads and lags are estimated to have made a difference of two billion dollars to the balance of payments, and the weakness of the lira is obviously caused by this and other actions stemming from lack of confidence rather than from any fundamental weakness of the Italian economy.

The reverse would seem to be true in the case of Switzerland, where the strength of the Swiss franc is not caused by any spectacular performance of the Swiss economy by itself. The balance of trade remains, of course, an element of fundamental importance for the value of any currency, but its impact, and particularly the effect of changes in the balance of trade, appears to be relatively smaller than heretofore, and slower in making itself felt in the monetary situation of a country.

WORLD TRADE

In spite of these very real difficulties, however, world trade has continued to grow vigorously. According to the I.M.F. it has increased by 18% in 1972 (compared with 12·1% in 1971) to reach a record volume of $760 billion. During the last ten years, the volume has tripled, and during the last twenty years it has increased five times. Half of the growth of 1972 has, it must be admitted, been due to price increases which have themselves been strongly influenced by the devaluation of the dollar. This has caused a tremendous increase in the foreign trade figures of countries other than the United States, when expressed in dollars. Nevertheless, the real increase of world trade has been 9% in 1972, and that is still an unusually high growth rate.

The superficial conclusion must be, therefore, that, in spite of increasing costs and complications owing to monetary disturbances, international trade has been able to grow strongly, thereby proving its inventiveness and adaptability. But I would add that this has been true 'for the time being', and that it has sometimes been made possible by the existence of certain escape routes in the form of alternative methods of financing which the banks were still in a position to offer.

THE EURO-CURRENCY MARKET

The most important of these opportunities has been provided by the existence of the euro-currency market. Its functioning has been discussed at such length that I do not feel the need to spend much time on it now. But I would like to emphasize the role this free international monetary market is playing in the financing of world trade because that is an aspect which somctimes seems to be underestimated. Of course, ordinary imports and exports of raw materials, agricultural produce and most manufactured goods are still handled in the customary manner of documentary letters of credit or on open account. In all these instances credits are basically arranged between banks and their own customers, either in their own currency or in a foreign currency which normally can be sold or bought forward so as to avoid exchange exposure. This, of course, goes on today as before, but there are three respects in which the present monetary instability affects the efficiency of the operation and leads to costly and complicated arrangements.

1. Long-term planning in exports becomes much more difficult if rates of exchange are completely uncertain and unpredictable. This will, in some instances, lead to a reduction in exports, but more often it will simply attract additional costs.

2. Protection against possible exchange losses has become more expensive. An exporting company may either go into continuing forward exchange operations or attract medium-term loans in the currencies in which its exports are denominated. This latter method may, however, be restricted or even completely forbidden by the foreign exchange regulations of the exporter's monetary authorities.

3. A multinational company may be severely obstructed in its cash-management by the uncertainties in the foreign exchange field, which may force it to go into leads and lags operations.

PROTECTING INTERNATIONAL TRADE

We now come to our second question: How to protect international trade against the damaging influence of monetary instability?

The problem can be approached from two sides: by trying to

determine the way in which national and international authorities should solve the monetary problem, or by indicating ways in which private companies can adapt to a situation of continuing instability. The first approach is both outside the scope of this paper and beyond the grasp of its author. Nevertheless, a few remarks might be permitted. The first requirement is the definition of the problem. Strange as it may seem, this has not yet been achieved. Some years ago, economists were of the opinion that the problem was to maintain sufficient international liquidity to cope with the growth of world trade.

Today the problem clearly is one of excess liquidity and how to reduce its—largely inflationary—effects. Thus the fundamental problem might be defined as 'the *management* of international liquidity'. Clearly not even an attempt is made to achieve this at present: the most countries do is to control liquidity at home for the purpose of internal economic stability.

A second remark concerns the float. In the absence of fixed parities the question can be asked whether a clean float does not provide the best basis for world trade. In theory, a system of freely floating exchange rates should have a stabilizing influence, since a strong demand for a country's products on account of its currency being undervalued would lead to a rise in the parity of that currency and thereby to a reduction in the demand for the country's products.

A dirty float, on the other hand, in which countries manipulate the rates of their currencies to obtain advantages for their exports, will inevitably disturb and thereby hamper the developments of international trade. But wild fluctuations—however clean they may be—upset and disrupt international trade for the reasons mentioned above. One is forced to conclude, therefore, that a certain minimum of dirt will have to be built into the float in most circumstances.

CENTRAL BANK INTERVENTION

Intervention by central banks in the foreign exchange markets, not for the purpose of promoting their own country's exports but in order to safeguard a certain amount of stability in the international foreign exchange market, will, moreover, have a beneficial effect by improving the climate for international trade.

In this context, the joint float of a number of European currencies vis-à-vis the dollar is a highly significant development. So far, i.e. since 19 March of this year when it was instituted, it has worked well, and with some optimism one may regard it as the beginning of that monetary union which must, by 1980, be the final achievement of the European Economic Community. It is difficult to see, however, how the present snake without a tunnel could survive a situation of severe discrepancy between the balance of payments situations of its participants unless there were a strong European Monetary Fund to back it up.

TWO-TIER MARKETS

A third remark I would like to make concerns two-tier markets. This concept includes a number of systems which have in common a partial fixation of exchange rates. Generally speaking, transactions of a commercial nature are carried out under a system of fixed parities, whereas non-commercial transactions are carried out on the so-called 'financial' market of freely floating rates. In other words, the monetary authorities intervene only to protect the exchange rate which is used for commercial transactions. The countries which apply this system at present, Belgium, France and Italy, however, do not make the same distinction between commercial and financial transactions—transfers on account of tourism or salaries, for instance, do not belong to the same category in each of these countries—but it is safe to say that the bulk of payments stemming from imports and exports of goods and most services are covered by the commercial market and therefore carried out under a system of fixed parities. The system has been widely discussed and it has its strong advocates and antagonists. Those who are in favour can point out that certainly in Belgium, where it has been in force ever since the war, and also in France, it has worked well and seems to have given considerable stability to the monetary system. It gives greater security to international trade than a complete float, and is easier for the monetary authorities to maintain than completely fixed parities.

Those who are against the system—and they are mainly to be found in countries which have never tried it—point out that it requires a rather cumbersome system of foreign exchange control, and that even so it is not safe against fraud, which will become more tempting as the margin between the controlled commercial rate and the free rate widens.

Furthermore they object to the two-tier market system because it would damage the efficiency of important financial centres such as London and Frankfurt.

It is not the purpose of this paper to go into these somewhat academic controversies. If we can achieve a new world monetary system with fixed parities soon, or even if such a system can be devised and maintained within the European Economic Community, there will be little need to introduce the two-tier system on a general scale. If these efforts were to break down, however, and I am sorry to say that such a disappointing outcome cannot be completely discarded, some kind of two-tier system might gain new adherents. They could then point out that whereas a temporary float may be the best system to arrive at new fixed parities, a permanent float will have a damaging effect on trade, and may lead to the highly disruptive type of competitive exchange-rate wars of the thirties which will result in strict controls being introduced anyway. In order to avoid that most undesirable situation, a system of fixed rates for commercial transactions only—which would give no shelter to speculative short-term capital movements—might well have its attractions, particularly from the point of view of international trade finance. In short, I would not exclude it as a second-best solution.

PROTECTION AGAINST MONETARY INSTABILITY

Having made these general remarks on the present situation, I should now like to discuss the different protective instruments available to international trade in a period of monetary instability. In the first place there is, of course, the forward exchange market. For periods up to one year it is functioning well, particularly in London and, if I may say so without undue pride, also in Amsterdam. In those two centres at least there are no restrictions imposed on forward transactions, for residents or non-residents. In Amsterdam there is a daily official quotation of forward rates of all the leading international currencies for periods up to six months, enabling customers to control the service of the banks.

To give an idea of the increase in the foreign exchange operations caused without any doubt by the present monetary instability, my bank is today carrying out twice as many forward transactions as one year ago. In a number of other markets, such as Paris, Milan and Stockholm, restrictions are imposed on forward operations, both as regards periods and the type of transactions to be covered, and this makes it that much more difficult for companies in those countries to protect themselves against exchange losses.

Secondly, there is the operation of leads and lags described briefly above. This is, of course, not only a method to diminish or avoid exposures in weak currencies and to benefit from positions in currencies which are considered to be a candidate for revaluation. It is also a means of mitigating the effect of credit restrictions imposed by national authorities. By shortening the credit terms on his exports, and lengthening the terms of payments on his imports, an exporter established in a country which has imposed credit restrictions may reduce his dependence on internal credit.

A company operating with a number of subsidiaries or affiliates in different countries can decide in which country it wants to increase or reduce the utilization of bank credit, taking into account these different elements. But also a company dealing with regular trading partners in different countries can make arrangements with them concerning speedier payments, concentration of excess funds in convertible accounts and other conditions which sometimes can lead to a better use of credit facilities, greater safety against exchange risks, or both.

These different methods are being increasingly applied on a more systematic and sophisticated basis and with the use of computers. They are generally described as 'cash-management'. In many instances they lead to considerable economies in the operations of companies engaged in international trade.

Cash-management is applied to short-term transactions, as the name indicates. Medium- and long-term trade financing has to rely on other methods to obtain safety and efficiency. It is here that the euro-currency market is providing valuable service.

In the first place it makes it possible to cover longer-term receivables in weak currencies by longer-term debt in those same currencies. If this is done on a roll-over basis, which means that the interest rate is fixed every three or six months on the basis of the London inter-bank rate, it has the additional advantage of allowing the borrower to decide at the end of each interest fixing date whether to utilize or not to utilize the facility or to terminate it.

Furthermore, the loan agreement may provide for the possibility of utilizing the facility in different convertible currencies, depending on the requirements of the borrower and the availability of the particular currency in the market. In this way a borrower may switch from indebtedness in dollars to

Deutschmarks or guilders in accordance with his needs for that particular currency and for a period determined by him. Unfortunately, the system does not work flawlessly. In the first place, the banks granting the facility will have to include an availability clause in the loan agreement since they cannot undertake to provide any required currency at any future moment. Secondly, interest rates in the euro-currency market fluctuate freely, and it is therefore not possible to determine the cost of the facility over any length of time. Of course, utilization can be terminated when it becomes too expensive, but this also depends on the borrower's liquidity or his alternative borrowing possibilities. Finally, and this is the most severe drawback, national authorities may prevent their citizens from borrowing abroad, by imposing exchange restrictions, reserve requirements or other means, thereby blocking their access to the euro-currency market.

UNWANTED DOLLARS

In western Europe such measures were taken in many countries in order to stem the influx of unwanted dollars, and one may hope that they will be of a temporary nature.

Unfortunately, however, the desire to somehow control or at least restrict the free functioning of the euro-currency market will probably be haunting monetary authorities for quite some time, and there is little reason to believe that barriers and restrictions to the free flow of capital will soon be abandoned. Even so, it is my firm belief that our highly interdependent and complex international economic system will not be able to operate without an international money market and that the euro-currency market—which simply is another name for the same thing—will continue to function and to render valuable services.

The Role of the Banks

In concluding let me make a few observations about the activity of financial institutions serving international trade. One of the essential qualities of the banking profession is flexibility and inventiveness, and those who prove to be lacking in those qualities will sooner or later be by-passed by competitors who offer quicker, cheaper or more comprehensive services to their clients. The strong competitiveness of banking, particularly in a period of high international liquidity, tends to reduce profitability, however, and this may sometimes lead to the acceptance of greater risks.

In trade financing this latter tendency has been showing itself in the acceptance of longer terms and weaker borrowers than would have been considered only a few years ago. On the other hand, one must admit that the dynamic growth of world trade and the enormous investments required for the development of natural resources and infrastructure do require far greater efforts from financial institutions, both as regards the amounts involved and the geographical area to be covered. This situation has stimulated the establishment of specialized organizations, often backed up by a group of large banks, engaged in medium-term lending and international capital market operations of considerable magnitude. During the last five years some of these finance companies have grown in size far beyond anything that was expected at the time of their founding. Their strength lies not only in their powerful shareholders and in the expertise they have acquired, but also in the fact that, as a joint venture, they can sometimes accept risks which each individual shareholder-bank might hesitate to take.

On the other hand, groups of banks from different countries have joined forces by establishing common operations in third countries and by granting combined credit facilities to multinational customers. In doing all these things they have followed the requirements of the market and at the same time stimulated the international operations of their industrial and commercial clients.

Jointly and individually, many banks have, furthermore, increased the range of their services by introducing not only new types of credit such as euro-currency roll-overs, multi-currency global credit lines and international leasing facilities, but also entirely new services such as cash-management. It seems justified to conclude that, in spite of present disturbances, the financial community is playing a constructive role in furthering international trade, and that it is in the interest of both the developed and the developing parts of the world that it should continue to do so in the greatest possible freedom.

Personal Finance and Services

by M. G. Wilcox, M.B.E., F.I.B.

I. Introduction

1. THE SUBJECT AND ITS TREATMENT

For a participant in an international conference of this scope, there is a natural tendency to encounter problems of definition. However, I have been fortunate in receiving a subject which can I think be easily identified as referring entirely to services provided for people in their capacity as personal customers.

But there is less certainty when we come to consider what type of institution is providing these services and in this connection I feel that some declaration by me is called for.

Quite evidently, I must think of banks and banking in the widest sense of those expressions, but only so far as their activities apply to the individual.

My paper, therefore, concerns banks and banking groups in contact with the community through branches and retail offices of various kinds. In some countries most or all the services to which I refer are—or would be—provided by departments within a single institution; in others—like the United Kingdom—some facilities are to be found in separate subsidiary or associated companies, sometimes for legal or regulatory reasons and sometimes as a matter of administrative convenience. At all events my reference to a 'bank' should be taken as equally meaning a 'banking group' if such is locally more relevant.

I propose to structure my paper in this way:

I—an *introduction* to the subject from the standpoint of both banker and customer, indicating the expectations of each;

II—an examination of *developments in the United Kingdom* in recent years;

III—a brief survey of *trends in developed countries* generally;

IV—*the prospects for change.*

The final point which I would make by way of introduction is that I shall inevitably include in this paper a great deal that is already known to individual readers. I hope that such material will be allowed on the ground that a broadly-based survey may be useful for reference and the basis of debate.

2. THE IMPORTANCE OF PERSONAL ACCOUNT BUSINESS TO COMMERCIAL BANKS

In a free enterprise economy there can be only one basic reason for commercial banks to provide facilities for personal customers —or any other facilities for that matter—namely the creation of profit, either directly or indirectly. Here in the United Kingdom there is a tendency to regard national branch banking as something akin to a public service—and I do not doubt that similar attitudes exist elsewhere. That viewpoint can perhaps be seen as an open recognition of the fundamental importance of banking to the community and a quiet tribute to its reliability —for example, in the provision of cash and in payment transmission activities—but although there is a strong sense of social responsibility in the way in which a banker seeks to conduct his business, he must have regard to the reasonable expectations of the shareholders.

In fact any view of the market will show that the personal

customer is an increasingly important part of the banking scene and relevant to each of these business objectives:

(*a*) *The need to collect deposits*

We would all agree that deposits are overwhelmingly the most significant element in the trading resources of a bank and the accumulated moneys on personal accounts—as distinct from corporate or other accounts—constitute an important proportion of the whole. Indeed, in the United Kingdom, over half the demand and seven-day deposits obtained through branch banking systems come from non-corporate accounts. This reverses the situation which existed as recently as 1955, when business customers contributed over half of total current and deposit account balances.

Personal deposits, as well as having this importance in aggregate, have the further attribute that they are composed of a large number of relatively small amounts, and as a total these lodgements prove in practice to be a good deal more stable than the mercurial whims and fancies of mankind would suggest was possible. The fact is that those who have accepted the convenience of a bank account, and who are not amongst the relatively few current account customers who overdraw, need to have—indeed, for peace of mind like to have—some funds always available to cover casual commitments.

Moreover, the spread ensures that deposits accumulated in a district of current plenty can be used by the bank concerned for lending in areas where a net demand for money has arisen for economic or other reasons.

(*b*) *The need to spread fixed operating costs*

The assembly of deposits through the catchment areas of a branch banking system is an expensive matter. In consequence, every possible economy of scale must be employed to keep down costs, and the presence of a large number of customers is a natural background to the introduction of computer accounting and kindred measures designed to save labour. Thus, without the contribution of personal business towards overhead costs it would have been less easy to justify and establish mechanisms which are all important to the attraction and effective working of corporate accounts in the same banking system;

(*c*) *The desire to widen the banks' sources of income*

Interest differential banking, with industry and commerce as the main destination for variable rate lending, is, I imagine, the bedrock of the business of most commercial banks. However, it must be the continuing aim of the banker to reduce his dependence on that source of income, and the personal customer provides an attractive target in this respect.

Special lending arrangements can be created which are capable of producing an above-average return from the interest aspect, and in addition there are many opportunities for fee-earning services to be introduced and sold to the personal customer.

The cost of attracting and integrating a new customer's business into the administrative machinery of a modern commercial bank is a definable expense which must be set against the ensuing transaction income, but once in an account relationship with the bank he is, more significantly, an obvious source of continuing revenue and must be nurtured as such. Every new capture is thus a prospective part of tomorrow's profit, and it must be the bank's unchanging ambition to expand the income per capita by selling more services to each customer.

Moreover, as the banking groups grow in diversity, the initial point of contact with the organization will less frequently be the request at a branch to open a cheque or savings account. It may instead come through a contact with the travel department or a trusteeship. And perhaps in time it will be quite possible to use certain services—like automated payment transfer systems—without becoming a customer in the traditional sense.

It is thus apparent that as a provider of deposits and as a prospective user of services the individual, however introduced, is an increasingly important element in the banking scene.

3. THE NEEDS OF THE PERSONAL CUSTOMER

In looking at the needs of the personal customer, we must consider both what he expects from us and also what we can sell him which he does not yet realize he requires!

His needs, present and potential, can, I think, be contained under these headings:

(*a*) *Cash as such and facilities for making and receiving remittances*
The ready availability of cash and the existence of a reliable and widely-accepted system for transmitting payments are prime requirements of the ordinary customer. He sometimes needs cash but more often wishes to settle debt by the use of the cheque—with or without the aid of a guarantee card—or by the employment of a credit card. These things are basic.

(*b*) *Financial advice*
Some people find money problems in our modern society both complex and confusing, and they require reliable advice from a trustworthy source.

The respect accorded the typical commercial bank and the special position of the branch manager in the community provide many opportunities for the banker to fill this role. Hopefully, the advice he gives—and that provided by his specialist staff—will regularly produce profitable business for his bank, but an evident desire to maintain impartiality in the satisfaction of the customer's needs will be his real source of long-term earning potential. The creation of goodwill today is the best guarantee of sustained revenue.

(*c*) *Credit and debit relationships*
The prospective customer looks for a secure lodgement for his cash and remuneration for his savings. When he needs to

borrow, he will expect a ready opportunity to do this with the minimum of formality.

(d) Associated services

Extensive advertising has brought the bank customer to expect something beyond the basic money services which I have described. For example, he will look for the immediate and local provision of some at least of the facilities which he will hear about in the course of the financial counselling to which I have already made reference—like the ready opportunity to implement investment decisions involving shares, unit trust units and so on; or the choice of a bank as corporate executor or trustee; or the ability to deal with insurance matters through his banker.

Moreover, the customer will expect the same standard of performance, the same display of ethics and the same evidence of integrity as exist in the basic banking relationship, and the entire fulfilment of these expectations becomes more and more difficult as the services become more diverse.

The needs of the personal customer are thus numerous and increasing. Some are fundamental and are central to traditional banking activity—like deposit lodgement, borrowing and the transmission of funds. Some have grown around these basic elements as secondary demands or have been induced by the banker's claims of ubiquity. The personal customer looks for reliability, convenience, security and simplicity in his dealings with his branch, and we shall see the extent to which these requirements—plus a welcoming atmosphere—are being met within a relationship which is designed to bring profit to the bank.

All the evidence suggests that, if the commercial banks cannot satisfy such needs then, as the overlap between the activities of different types of financial institution becomes more apparent and more significant, there are new competitors who will.

II. Developments in the United Kingdom in recent years

4. INTRODUCTORY

A great deal has happened to alter the banking scene in the United Kingdom over the past few years, and I propose to review these developments—in so far as they affect the personal customer—under the following headings:

(a) *social and economic changes;*

(b) *changes in the political and business environment,* stemming in particular from official action designed to allow increasing competition;

(c) *change in the banks' approach to the whole question of marketing;*

(d) *the need for new staff attitudes;*

(e) *the organizational consequences of these changes.*

5. SOCIAL AND ECONOMIC CHANGES IN THE UNITED KINGDOM WHICH HAVE INFLUENCED THE ATTITUDE OF PEOPLE TO BANKS

This is the age of the consumer, and the fact is reflected in the increasing interest shown by banks in the private customer. Perhaps it would be interesting to look at some of the factors which have had a bearing on the situation:

(a) *Improvements in living standards*

Probably the most important influence has been concerned not so much with bringing banking to the people as bringing the people to banking.

If you do not have any money you do not need a bank—and the reverse is, for bankers, fortunately just as true, for increasing real income has brought increasing business. For example, the earnings of the average manual worker in the United Kingdom are four times their 1951 level—compared with a multiple of 2½ times for prices—so that there is here a genuine increase in income and in the disposable surplus. It is not surprising that in the same period the number of private customers in the banking system has risen significantly.

There has, also, been a tendency to move from weekly to monthly wage settlement and, with the repeal of those parts of the Truck Acts of the nineteenth century which forced employers to settle wages in cash, remuneration is often remitted by cheque or by direct credit to a bank, with a consequential need by the employee for lodgement and drawing facilities. The result has been to provide new potential for deposits, and fresh opportunities to bring the idea of personal banking to a wider audience.

(b) Changing personal attitudes towards borrowing

Looking back into history there seem to be two major influences which have tended to prevent people from undertaking borrowing commitments, namely 'moral' reasons and fear—although even the Victorians judged it proper and decent and safe to seek home ownership by means of the long-term mortgage loan.

But to many people the use of credit has been an admission of weakness or worse, and I for one was enjoined by my father not to yearn for something before I had saved enough to buy it. I could, of course, remark with some accuracy, if with equal cynicism, that this injunction was issued in advance of the inflationary experience of recent years which has certainly encouraged the creation of borrowing to purchase assets at current prices, whilst paying back in tomorrow's depreciated currency.

But there are other and more relevant reasons for people showing a greater willingness to commit themselves to debt repayment over a period, namely:

—the existence of a broader safety margin in net disposable income than was the case in earlier years—in other words the increasing spending power to which I have already referred;

—a greater awareness by the employer of his responsibilities to the individual—during times of illness for example; and the parallel effect of:

—state intervention in the context of job security, unemployment pay, sickness allowances and pensions.

All these bring that greater feeling of security which must precede any intelligent and responsible decision to borrow.

It is not unreasonable to say that the point has now been reached where the use of instalment credit—particularly for the purchase of motor cars and consumer durables—permits the average man to enjoy real improvements in his standard of living at an earlier time than would otherwise be the case; it also encourages regular saving—albeit in arrears rather than in advance of an asset purchase. May it be remarked parenthetically that the United States and Canada have taken this process further than most other countries—their instalment debt per head of the population being more than four times the equivalent figure for the United Kingdom. Admittedly there is evidence on the other side of the Atlantic of some personal over-commitment, but the cases are relatively of no great consequence and the lesson is clear, namely that in Europe, for example, we can expect to see per capita debt rise appreciably over the next few years.

(c) Changing personal attitudes to banks

The somewhat rigid class divisions of years gone by tended to have a demarcation effect in settling who had bank accounts and who did not. In consequence, the process of wealth redistribution and other influences on the social scene have made a great difference to personal attitudes in this regard, and banks are now being seen much more as institutions doing their best to be all things to all men. Their advertising shows this, and the attempt made to introduce a more friendly atmosphere into bank premises is also relevant.

However, we have a long way to go yet before the aversions of yesterday are finally overcome.

6. CHANGES IN THE UNITED KINGDOM POLITICAL AND BUSINESS ENVIRONMENT

Some of the most far-reaching changes in commercial banking in the United Kingdom in recent years have been occasioned by moves by the authorities and in particular those moves designed to increase competition. The discernible common thread which runs through these endeavours is the increasing emphasis which has been placed on control through market forces rather than by specific directives.

The following are the more significant developments which have affected personal financial services:

(*a*) *Report of the National Board for Prices and Incomes 1967*

Under the Prices and Incomes Act of 1966, a reference was made to the National Board for Prices and Incomes for enquiry into 'questions relating to the system and level of bank charges'.

The report was published in 1967 and, whilst concluding that bank commission charges were not in any way excessive, it nevertheless made a number of recommendations for increased competition between the banks, including:

(i) a joint renunciation by the clearing banks of their agreement on maximum deposit rates and minimum lending rates;

(ii) the prescription by the authorities of common reserve requirements for all banks and other financial institutions which would apply to capital resources and liquid assets in relation to total obligations and deposit liabilities respectively;

(iii) the disclosure of true profits and inner reserves by all banks;

(iv) the abolition of collective agreements between clearing banks concerning certain types of commission charge and the publication of a tariff in respect of standard transactions;

(v) the introduction of more flexible and competitive arrangements covering branch opening hours.

It is of interest to note that almost all these recommendations have effectively been adopted or are matters under active consideration at the present time.

An important side result of the enquiry was to discover that, in contrast to popular belief, the authorities were prepared to consider giving their blessing to the amalgamation of major clearing banks. It had long been thought—ever since the Colwyn Committee reported in 1918 in fact—that such mergers would not be approved, but it became apparent that the policy had changed, as was proved in a practical way when National Provincial Bank and Westminster Bank joined in 1968, and Barclays Bank acquired Martins Bank in 1969.

(*b*) *The arrival of the Giro*

In 1968, the decision of H.M. Government to introduce a Giro system for payment transmission was implemented by the Post Office.

The service is conducted entirely on a credit-account basis, but in April 1970 arrangements were made for Giro customers to apply to a major finance house for personal loan facilities. This facility has since been extended.

The most recently available information suggests that in March 1973 there were 473,000 Giro account holders—which, of course, includes commercial customers—producing some £75 million of deposits, compared with £20,000 million in the clearing bank groups at the same date.

Without doubt, the arrival of the Giro had a competitive stimulus so far as the banks were concerned, and they have not treated its existence with anything approaching complacency. It is nevertheless true that the Giro has not achieved the degree of acceptance which kindred systems enjoy in other European countries. This is because the banks have for many years encouraged personal accounts—though not with the same intensity as has been seen in recent times—

and, in consequence, the use of the current account for payment transmission has become well established.

However, the Giro will doubtless continue to attract custom and its existence will, in a number of ways, be a continuing stimulus to the banks in the context of personal business. Whether over a period the banks will seek to acquire customers in exactly the same market has yet to be decided.

(*c*) *Voluntary disclosure of profits and inner reserves*

Beginning with the financial year 1969, the clearing banks discarded voluntarily the privilege given them by the Companies Acts over many years of making undisclosed transfers to inner reserves and, in consequence, concealing in absolute terms the true nature of their profits and overall financial condition.

The effect of this move was to sharpen still further the competitive attitude of the banks whose individual and relative performances were now known to the world, and in particular to those who seek to assess such matters in the market place for stocks and shares.

(*d*) *The Bank of England's proposals on Competition and Credit Control* 1971

The rigid system of ceiling controls for banking institutions had long been seen in the City of London as inequitable and the enemy of innovation, for it had a deadening influence on inventiveness and enthusiasm far beyond the boundaries of loans and overdrafts.

In May 1971, the Bank of England, in a paper styled **'Competition and Credit Control',** acknowledged the shortcomings of past methods and proposed new arrangements which were designed to influence the overall quantity of credit in the financial system at any one moment, whilst permitting individual institutions some opportunity to reap the rewards of relative efficiency.

Since October 1971, all banks and finance houses of significant size have been involved in these new control methods, which are applied in a broadly uniform way and are essentially traditional in character. They depend for their effect on minimum liquidity requirements, involving the maintenance of a proportion of assets in a defined and in practice a low-yielding form, with in addition unscheduled demands for 'special deposits' to be placed with the central bank at rates of interest which are highly unattractive when measured against the return on other interest-earning assets.

This is not the place to develop detail, but it is relevant to the subject matter of this paper:

—that direct quantitative controls on lending have been abandoned, and the authorities are now dependent almost entirely on their ability to influence the money supply through, inter alia, the action they take to make the price of credit in the banking system either more or less attractive to the borrower;

—that, after a transitory period when banks are adjusting to the new environment, fiercer competition for personal deposits is likely to occur;

—that lending policies will be designed so as to deploy resources amongst different types of customer in a more planned and positive manner and the relative importance of the personal sector will thus fall to be reviewed;

—that the banks will certainly take an increased interest in consumer credit, and will be less inclined to leave so much of this to the finance houses and similar providers of funds for routine purposes, including car purchase, home improvement and kindred outlays. In consequence, and with this increased freedom of choice, they are not likely in future to let their lendings to personal customers fall away quite so far as they did for example in the 1960s. They should, henceforth, be able always to find some funds for lending on such accounts and, whilst these advances would, in tight money conditions, be expensive, history suggests that potential borrowers will still be there.

Not surprisingly, the authorities have made it plain that they may wish to give 'qualitative' guidance from time to time—within which could be included any words of influence they wished to issue on the amount of consumer credit made available by the banking system. However, the personal borrower has become a much more important element in bank lending in the past two years, and it seems unlikely that any official guidance will totally unseat him from that enhanced situation.

(*e*) *The deposit and repayment period concerned with instalment credit contracts*

In July 1971, the government removed the controls which concerned the terms allowed on hire purchase business, and which in practice also influenced those on other instalment credit facilities associated with goods. For example, it was no longer necessary in law for a hire purchase contract to require that not less than a stated proportion of the cost of a motor car acquired with the aid of the financial institution in question should be found by the user of the vehicle, or that he should discharge the debt within a specified period of time.

This freedom for each lender to offer terms of his choosing has rebounded to the advantage of the customer in that competition for his business has been further stimulated.

(*f*) *Crowther Committee on Consumer Credit* 1971

This committee was established by H.M. Government to review the whole subject of consumer credit. Its views and recommendations—which have been widely supported in their general intent—included the following:

—the desirability of encouraging competition between credit-granting institutions of all sorts;

—the removal of artificial legal barriers between different types of accommodation—notably hire purchase, credit sale and ordinary lending;

—the likelihood that personal credit facilities would tend in future to rely less on the security of goods—for the purchase of which the accommodation would in typical circumstances have been granted—and more on an assessment of the creditworthiness of the borrower; an increasing need for adequate and accurate credit information would clearly flow from such a trend;

—the need to provide further protection for the consumer, by ensuring, for example, that he was provided with all the information—such as true rates of interest—which he needed in order to make a choice between competing forms and sources of credit.

No part of the committee's recommendations has yet become law, but a voluntary code encompassing many of the 'truth-in-lending' proposals has been adopted by the banks pending the consumer protection legislation which is expected next year.

(*g*) *Younger Committee on privacy* 1972

Public concern regarding the implications for the individual of computer-based data systems was one of the matters mentioned in the report of this committee.

Moreover, the report suggested that the banks should be placed on implied, if not direct, notice that future developments in the use of information systems touching the creditworthiness of an individual would have to be examined from social as well as commercial points of view.

(*h*) *Anti-inflationary measures* 1973

Inflation is the enemy of saving. It is not surprising, therefore, that the current policies of H.M. Government include much emphasis on the desirability of removing those inhibitions against saving which grow from the legitimate belief that money which depreciates is not worth keeping. If successful, there should be an increasing flow of private savings in which the banks will wish to share.

Moreover, fresh efforts are being made in the United

Kingdom at the present time to control prices. A 'voluntary' ceiling on prices for services was introduced last year to which the banks subscribed, and this has now been incorporated in legislation. The overall effect will be to hasten the impact of competition upon operating efficiency, since productivity at branch level is crucial to bank profit performance.

7. CHANGES IN THE APPROACH TO MARKETING

The changes which have occurred in recent years in the environment in which the United Kingdom banks are operating have had their influence on marketing methods—indeed they have pointed to the need for the banks to be infinitely more positive in this regard than they have ever been before.

The general attitude in the past has been for the banker to wait in his parlour for the customer to call, in something akin to the role of supplicant. Now it is accepted that bank services must be sold like any other product.

The banker must be sensitive to changing public demand and to the aspirations of the individual, whether they concern a desire to obtain new assets or enjoy new services. Fresh and tempting products must be introduced, but equally it must be expected that some will be removed from the range from time to time—indeed it may well be that the concept of the product life cycle so evident in other industries will assume increasing importance in banking, especially in regard to new types of saving schemes and new ways of borrowing.

This revolutionary approach to selling has also had an influence on the actual content and role of press advertising. One now sees less of the general prestige advertising which was concerned more with emphasizing the eminence of the bank than the nature of its product. The tendency now is to point advertising at a specific sector of the population, giving meaningful information about a single service. Thus, with more and more evidence of name recognition, and an increasing tendency for the ordinary man to take an interest in bank advertising, one must expect him, on seeing some display in which a bank claims greatness, to ask that the next announcement should demonstrate how that greatness can be used to his advantage—and today!

On specific marketing matters this can be said:

(*a*) *competition for the personal customer*

Few established personal customers move their accounts from one bank to another, so that the capture of the customer in the first instance is all-important.

This truth is very apparent in the United Kingdom, where considerable effort is made by every bank to ensure that they get at least an adequate and hopefully a growing share of the accounts of young people. As they move from school to university or to some other college of further education, they can expect to be wooed by the banks with promises of commission-free accounts for the years before full-time employment. And to demonstrate how important the banks consider the university undergraduate as an investment for the future, it is increasingly likely that he will find a branch conveniently situated on the campus, or as close as may be practicable.

Sponsorship of sport and the arts in ways which bring the name of a bank to the notice of the younger generation is another evidence of this desire to achieve a customer relationship early in adult life.

Branches are also to be found in large office and factory premises, where it is hoped to acquire accounts and thus a captive market for a variety of services. In the siting of these and other new branches and in their physical attributes one can discern the same theme, namely to present an attractive face to someone who is thinking of an account for the first time.

(*b*) *The introduction of new payment services*

The importance to the customers of a convenient, simple and accurate payments transmission system has been indicated in what has gone before, and in relatively recent years we have, of course, seen these developments as additional to the established *standing order* and *credit transfer* systems:

—*direct debiting*, where—by agreement—the creditor initiates regular debits to the account of a personal customer;

—*cheque cards* to improve the acceptability of the cheque in retail situations; in recent years extended as a cashing medium through the Eurocheque scheme;

—*cash dispensers*—with the latest version capable of being linked to the customer's account on a computer-based book-keeping system and able to make note deliveries of varying amount—have been installed at bank branches throughout the country. The main purpose of the existing installations is to provide cash outside banking hours, but the customer whose only requirement is a simple package of money can obtain this at any time without entering the branch office. The capital costs are substantial, but we can expect these useful machines to appear also in railway stations, airports, department stores and the like.

—a bank-based *credit card* can now be obtained from each of the major institutions and the use made of this facility increases daily. At present the cards in question—BARCLAYCARD and ACCESS—are primarily shoppers' cards for relatively small transactions, with the latter restricted at present to a limited geographical area. But their use, both in terms of the type of transaction for which they are accepted and the territories within which they can be employed, will clearly expand.

(*c*) *The provision of new types of borrowing arrangement*

The overdraft has traditionally been the way in which most personal borrowing needs have been satisfied in the banking system, and it remains an important facility for those who wish to set up an arrangement which will cover their occasional needs on the most advantageous interest terms.

The personal loan—for disciplined repayment by instalments—has been with us for some fifteen years, and has gained new prominence in the considerable expansion of personal lending which has occurred since the autumn of 1971. Moreover, it is likely to be seen in a fresh form in the future as banking by post is used to an increasing extent. Dealing with a postal application for an unsecured loan requires a change in managerial approach but, with the growing use of credit-scoring techniques, which can be refined in the handling of thousands of conventional personal loan applications, the operation becomes easier.

However, the facilities likely to be used on an increasing basis in the future are *revolving credit* arrangements available directly through the banks or by using the services of their credit card companies. These have the attribute—shared with the traditional overdraft facility—that they constitute a source of credit which can be used continuously without a fresh consultation with the bank. Apart from simple questions of convenience, the average customer is not fond of presenting himself as an applicant for credit more often than he must, and these schemes please him by the general avoidance of this formality.

The mechanics of the two systems are these:

(i) *Revolving credit facilities*

These are in essence continuous borrowing arrangements which are provided to the personal customer for use whenever and for whatever purpose he decides; typical conditions would include:

—drawings on the borrowing account up to the agreed limit may be effected at any time in multiples of, say, £50 by transfer to a current account;

—a standing-order monthly transfer of a minimum of 1/30 of the agreed loan limit is made from current account to the borrowing account to provide for progressive repayment;

—the account on which the loan is taken may thus in

practice move into credit—when some interest is paid to the customer—but is, more usually, in debit, when a flat rate of interest is levied at six monthly intervals;
—free life cover is customarily provided for borrowers up to the age of sixty.

Thus for the borrower the need to renegotiate a fresh loan for each new requirement is removed. In addition, the fixed monthly payment continues to reduce any outstanding indebtedness, and when full repayment is achieved it can transform the account into a repository for regular savings.

(ii) *Credit card*

It is believed that this facility will, to a large extent, eventually supplant other forms of credit used at the point of sale. Basically the system is, of course, from the accounting standpoint, an alternative method of money transmission which is concerned primarily with the settlement of debt in shops and other retail establishments, but a built-in revolving credit facility is an important adjunct. For convenience, perhaps I could summarize its features, which typically might be these:

—a credit card may be presented as a means of payment to, for example, any retailer, mail order house or provider of services who is a participant in the scheme; the trader usually displays a sign to this effect;
—an identifying bill or debit note covering the transaction is raised by using the card in a special imprinting machine;
—the retailer will customarily credit his ordinary current account with this bill, which will be considered by his bank as cash from the date of its receipt, subject to a small deduction representing a service charge by the credit card company;
—the cardholder, who joins the scheme free of charge, is sent a regular statement of his account with the credit card company, usually on a monthly basis, showing the payments outstanding;

—from receipt of this account the cardholder has twenty-five days during which the debit may be extinguished without charge; beyond this period interest—usually at $1\frac{1}{2}\%$ per month—is applied from the date of the statement;

—a maximum borrowing or credit limit is agreed with each cardholder, who undertakes to make a monthly payment to the credit card company of a minimum of 5% of the amount outstanding;

—a cash loan may be obtained by a cardholder up to the amount of his available credit limit at any of the bank branches participating in the scheme; such advances, however, bear interest from the moment they are taken until they are repaid and this rate is usually the same as for sales vouchers, i.e. $1\frac{1}{2}\%$ per month; alternatively, they may be treated as sales vouchers but with a commission charge levied at the time of encashment.

It is apparent that this scheme, particularly when applied to consumer purchases, has many convenient attributes for both the customer and the bank. Not the least of these are the reduction in the number of individual transactions on the account, and the easier administration of small borrowings for personal customers.

In both of these areas, increasing simplicity must mean a reduction in staff costs and, hopefully, of the service charge to the customer.

(*d*) *Other new services* have been introduced in the move towards branch offices able to offer a comprehensive 'one stop banking' style service and with the parallel objective of raising the revenue of each retail outlet.

8. THE NEED FOR NEW STAFF ATTITUDES AND TRAINING

To meet the changing market conditions of recent years it has been necessary to encourage a new approach by staff to the fulfilment of their work, and in this context these matters are of relevance:

(*a*) *Sales training* is now a formal educational process in many banks. Such might include, for example, guiding branch managers or reorganizing business development opportunities or securities department staff on ways in which they can interest a customer in other services.

(*b*) *Work study techniques* are increasingly of relevance to the development of an effective sales staff, and some major banks in the United Kingdom have made considerable progress in studies on these lines. Perhaps the most obvious instance of this activity concerns counter staff, where improvements in the method of cash handling can bring significant benefits in time saving, and thus in customer contentment. Operational research is, of course, a related subject.

9. THE WIDENING MARKET—ORGANIZATIONAL CHANGES AND ADMINISTRATION

The widening of the range of activities regarded as in or near the banking function has resulted not unnaturally in the formation of fresh specialist departments or the addition—by creation or share purchase—of new subsidiary or associated companies, when this method of extension seemed more apt or was made necessary by official attitude or regulation. In consequence group structures have tended to develop, with separate divisions or companies dealing with different activities or sectors of the market. For example, stakes in finance houses were acquired to give the banks an interest in hire purchase; insurance broking businesses have been established to take advantage of the selling possibilities of the customer catchment area; unit trust management companies have been created or acquired as this method of holding funds has become more popular with the private investor; and one bank now owns a major shareholding in a travel and tour-operating business with world-wide connections.

Initially, the object of such initiatives was to provide services complementary to those historically available in order to meet a widening demand. However, the influence of the authorities on the behaviour of financial institutions has had an even more profound effect and has, for example, tempted finance houses into commercial banking, induced clearing banks to provide instalment credit of a nature and to a market sector which was previously the preserve of the finance houses and created a new interest in merchant banking. Where the various elements of a banking group used to be largely complementary they can now be competitive; and subsidiaries sometimes compete against their parent bank and vice versa.

10. 1967 TO 1973—A SUMMARY OF DEVELOPMENTS

The developments seen in these years can be summarized thus:

(*a*) *a general improvement in the standard of living* has encouraged the use of the personal services of commercial banking groups as a convenient method of making payments; as a relatively cheap source of personal credit—mostly for consumer goods; and as an increasingly attractive depository for small savings;

(*b*) *the central authorities have instituted radical reforms, which encourage competition* and which return to the banks much initiative in allocating resources to various parts of the economy, including the personal sector;

(*c*) *public debate about the responsibility of corporations to the consumer* has been encouraged by official action;

(*d*) the personal customer, neglected during many years of stringent monetary control, has become a *primary source of business interest and potential revenue;*

(*e*) *increased competition for personal business* has produced a spate of new services, and greater demands upon staff skills and bank administration.

III. Trends in developed countries

11. THE FORM AND STRUCTURE OF BANKS AND BANKING GROUPS

An examination of the retail banking system in western countries reveals much diversity in ownership, structure and branch organization.

In some countries—for example France and Italy—there are state-owned institutions carrying on much the same sort of multi-branch and nationwide business as do the public company equivalents in Scandinavia or Switzerland or the United Kingdom.

The United States currently presents another picture, with major commercial banks restricted to a state, a city or even—as in Illinois—a single physical situation.

In some countries the personal customer and the corporate customer are equally at home in the same office, whilst in others it is apparent that the ordinary citizen tends to find the savings bank or its near equivalent a more congenial and obvious site for his custom, letting the company client remain paramount in the still awesome halls of the banque d'affaires and the large commercial banking institutions.

Then again, a complete service for personal customers is sometimes provided by the bank itself and sometimes—for legal or other reasons—by a subsidiary or associated company.

But a closer look demonstrates that, taken overall, the banking systems of these various countries are being influenced by similar changes in the environment in which they operate—the differences are not so much in nature as in degree—and their posture to personal banking also shows considerable similarity.

12. SOCIAL DEVELOPMENTS

Everywhere the increasing strength of the individual in business relationships is becoming apparent. Perhaps the tendency is most obvious in the United States where, speaking in the most general terms, the growing sense of social responsibility in the major corporation is paralleled by the effective work of the consumer activists with their powerful lobby in political places.

But similar developments are to be seen in E.E.C. countries where, for example, moves to harmonize consumer credit law are likely to lay special stress on consumer protection.

Again, in Japan, the National Livelihood Council—which advises the Prime Minister—is calling for a greater participation by consumers in governmental advisory organs dealing with financial and banking problems.

Truth in lending legislation had its origins in the United States, but similar moves have since been made in many lands. The same comment could be made regarding laws to regulate credit information bureaux and in the insurance of deposits.

13. GROWTH OF COMPETITION

We have seen that, in the United Kingdom, the market in financial services has experienced some liberalization in recent years and similar developments are visible elsewhere.

In both France and Germany, radical reforms were introduced in the late sixties to improve competition. Decrees in France transformed the regulation of credit interest rates on savings accounts and fixed deposits, allowed banks to extend their retail networks and modernized credit arrangements. Controls on branching had been removed in Germany by 1958, but it took until 1967 before the authorities relinquished the regulations on interest rates.

In Canada the decennial revision of the Bank Act which followed the report of a Royal Commission in 1964 has, amongst other things, prohibited interest rate agreements between the banks.

Then again, America's Hunt Commission Report, which was published in 1971, and which contains proposals for increasing competition within the financial system, is now being considered by the United States Administration. Informed opinion suggests that the general trend of its reasoning will be followed.

Widely, therefore, one finds a tendency for lines of demarcation between types of institution to be smudged or erased by official fiat or with official encouragement. Most often it is the private customer—historically and inevitably the weakest negotiator when standing alone against united interests—who is now likely to benefit from the greater competition between sectors of the market and between individual businesses which thus results.

14. THE WIDENING RANGE OF PERSONAL SERVICES

The growing attraction of the personal customer as a depositor, borrower and user of fee-earning services is reflected in the ever more visible attempts to acquire his—or her—business.

In Western Germany the commercial banks have moved towards 'all purpose' retail networks, with the distinction between various types of financial institution becoming less marked. As an instance of their versatility they are providing a broad spectrum of investment schemes, ranging from many types of unit trusts and property funds to 'investment packages' offering a choice of several different investment and savings schemes. In addition, several banks have established links with allied services, such as insurance facilities and investment advice. Others have developed travel subsidiaries and provide a broad range of tourist facilities including package holidays.

In the Netherlands, several kinds of personal loans and savings schemes are now provided on a national scale and many other services are also available—a guaranteed cheque facility, insurance of almost every kind, links with the stock market, the custody and administration of securities, financial advice and the management of personal assets. As in Germany, the banks are also moving into travel.

Similar trends can be discerned in the rest of Europe whilst, in Japan, the service given to customers is of a more personal nature than in some other countries, with more emphasis placed on customer-staff contact. The banks themselves are less forbidding and untypical furnishings, such as television sets, drinking-water machines and magazines, can often be found in an average Japanese branch. The variety of personal loans available has increased considerably in recent years and credit cards have also entered the scene. In addition, computerization has taken place on a large scale, with the banks offering an 'on-line' cash dispenser service.

The automatic deposit of employees' wages in banks is a growing trend in Japan, with 18% of companies in a recent sample saying that they had adopted the system and a further 8% expecting to use it shortly.

South Africa appears to be laying special stress on making branches attractive and much is done to establish personal relationships.

A similar trend is to be seen in the United States, where the allocation to a customer of a member of the staff in the role of 'personal banker' is an experiment which illustrates an intent to provide financial counselling on a continuing basis and seems to have had some success. Other services designed to assist the individual are pavement window cashier positions available after normal banking hours; the quick deposit box placed in the branch to receive credits without the need to visit a cashier and with the bank sending an acknowledgement by post; and more drive-in facilities.

In Australia, fresh and novel attempts are being made to recruit interest-bearing deposits from customers of all ages, and specially extended hours of opening are available within which savings account business can be transacted.

But as indicated earlier, the existence of Giro facilities in certain countries has, of course, an influence on the extent to which people use commercial banks for payments transmission.

15. THE DRIVE FOR PERSONAL SAVINGS

The scene is broadly the same in all developed countries. As examples, however, the savings of individuals in European countries in 1970 as a percentage of gross national product varied from under 6% for the United Kingdom to over 10½% for Belgium, with figures of 6½% for France, nearly 8% for Western Germany, 9% for Austria and 10% for the Netherlands. In money terms by far the largest volume of personal savings in these countries was recorded in Western Germany, followed by France and the United Kingdom.

Substantial real increases in the gross national products of all these countries are expected over the next few years but, more significantly, personal savings are likely to rise even faster. In consequence, there is keen competition amongst financial institutions, including housing associations, mutual funds and insurance companies, to acquire such savings, which it is estimated might double in money terms between 1970 and 1980. But erosion in the value of money remains an enemy to the desire to save and this aspect of national affairs is one of the factors influencing governments in their effort to combat inflation.

16. THE GROWTH IN CONSUMER CREDIT

It is widely accepted that in terms of direct earnings the banking activity in the personal sector which produces the most attractive return is lending in one form or another, and this is the area where banks generally have been looking for more custom.

The United States has not suffered from the social and moral inhibitions against borrowing which have been a typical feature of the European scene, and it has, moreover, enjoyed in relative terms the sharpest increase in living standards. In consequence, it has seen the biggest rise in consumer credit per head of population, followed by Canada and Australia. Statistics are not easy to obtain but, in 1967, the proportion of hire purchase and other instalment credit facilities to personal disposable income stood at 9·6 in the United States, 11·8 in Canada, 7·3 in Australia and only 4·2 in the United Kingdom.

Instalment credit was earlier the province of the finance companies but, in the United States and Canada, the banks made vigorous progress and for some years have been the paramount lenders in this field in the two countries.

In Europe—owing partly to legal hindrance or restrictions of official monetary policy—the growth of this type of business within banks has been slower and, as noted earlier, they chose first to enter the consumer credit industry by the purchase of equity stakes in finance houses, only later extending instalment loans themselves.

In Australasia, the tendency has been for progress to take the same route, whilst in South Africa it is notable that an institution which began its life as a finance house specializing in consumer credit is now a bank of considerable size.

17. GENERAL TRENDS

The trend everywhere is thus very similar, and can be summarized thus:

—*competition for the personal customer's* business shows in the increased standing of the consumer, the desire to acquire new deposits, and the introduction of numerous new services;

—the majority of countries are taking steps to combat inflation with varying amounts of success; this has particular relevance to the *continued attraction of personal savings;*

—*the expansion of consumer credit* continues at varying rates, providing banks with every encouragement to market new lending services.

IV. What changes will now be seen?

18. THE LIKELY AIMS OF THE BANKS IN THE CONTEXT OF PERSONAL FINANCE AND SERVICES

It is the duty of the management of every business undertaking to decide in which direction new investment should proceed in order to maximise sustainable profit, and in consequence the attitude of commercial banks to personal account facilities must be brought within the framework of profit planning. With strategy decided, the need to choose between alternatives remains, but I suggest that within its overall trading ambitions, the aims of a typical banking institution are likely to contain these objectives:

(*a*) to acquire and retain as wide and as numerous a clientele in the personal sector as possible, consistent with the efficient provision of personal banking services at a profit;

(*b*) to provide a cash and payment transfer service with national and international connections which embraces both cheque and credit card facilities; this implies a willingness and ability to meet investment costs of substantial amount;

(*c*) to hold an acceptable share of the market in personal deposits and in particular personal savings; but a simple account with simple interest will not always be enough;

(*d*) to provide consumer credit on terms which will ensure a volume of business sufficient to pay for administrative procedures which will increasingly be tolerable only if centralized as a means of achieving economy;

(*e*) to make such extensions into other forms of personal lending—such as housing finance—as is consistent with banking prudence and commercial viability;

(*f*) to create and market to personal customers—and non-customers in the sense that a continuing relationship may be absent—as wide a range of additional financial services as is compatible with the bank's view as to the desirable ambit of its activities.

19. THE CONSTRAINTS AND ENVIRONMENTAL INFLUENCES ON THE DEVELOPMENT OF PERSONAL ACCOUNT BUSINESS

We have seen that developments in personal banking in various countries in recent years show a marked similarity, which to a large degree is merely a reflection of similar experience in social and economic change. Parallel trends of this nature seem likely to continue and, whilst the pace and nature of change in one country may differ from those of its neighbour, there is for our purposes a sameness which can be a guide to new initiatives.

Socio-economic projections are notoriously inaccurate, but it seems reasonable to assume that in Europe for instance there will, over the next decade, be a gradual increase in employed persons—the source of our business. Moreover, there is a steady shift out of primary industries into service occupations, where the number of personal banking customers is highest. This trend is in line with experience in the United States, and is likely to result in about half the working population of Europe being so engaged by 1980.

As community occupations change, so do the demands of the people and the degree of their sophistication. Regions previously dependent on single activities—like mining or fishing—will become more diversified, with improved communications—for both people and knowledge—which will enable service industries to be decentralized from primary centres of population. Thus for the United Kingdom this must mean the greater need for and availability of sophisticated financial advice and services in provincial towns, and less day-to-day dependence on the capital.

Increasing affluence will bring greater opportunities to spend money on leisure pursuits and travel, a trend which is likely to be fastest in North America, Europe, Japan and Australasia. In areas where personal assets like the motor car are less in evidence—like South America and some Mediterranean countries—perhaps there will for a while be a concentration on affording and owning these symbols of a well equipped society.

I think it is also true that there will be increasing scope for competition between financial institutions—achieved in some instances by the reversal of legal restraints which have previously kept some businesses out of the field. Equally, it is my belief that the trend everywhere will be away from restrictive practices which have in the past had similar results.

And all this will support the tendency for the consumer to acquire a higher commercial standing with greater bargaining power and improvements in legal protection and redress.

But, finally, we must include in our thinking the cost factor, which is of significance to every bank as it feels the direct effect of increases in rents, in salaries and in the price of the goods and services it consumes.

20. POSSIBLE CHANGES IN BANKING ADMINISTRATION AND METHOD

The importance of the personal customer to the commercial banks—both now and increasingly in the future—has I think been established, and we must expect this factor to produce changes within the banking groups in a number of ways. It is inevitable that I should be influenced in my views by the prospects I see for banking in the United Kingdom, but I hope that the majority of these points will be accepted as having a wider relevance:

(*a*) *The role of the branch*

Tradition dies hard in Britain. The local branch is central to any commercial banker's approach to banking practice; to the customer it is the place where his account is maintained and the only normal channel of communication to the rest of the banking group beyond.

Modern technology is producing automated systems capable of handling all routine transactions through a central unit; personal accounts today are maintained at a spot most convenient for the Post Office. As a result the outlets of a multi-branch banking group are becoming first and foremost a chain of selling points not dissimilar to those found in other retail trades. Personal money services are the equivalent of products in any other main street business, and can be transacted at any convenient location.

Fortunately or unfortunately, however, the success of commercial branch banking is based upon personal relationships. Unlike the manufacturing process, people remain at the centre of our business. Impersonalizing the local service has its dangers, and it is in recognizing to what extent the branch business can be handled by automated means or by remote specialist support staff rather than by the ubiquitous branch manager and his staff, that the extent of the bank representation and the cost of its services can be planned.

(*b*) *The position of the branch manager*

The primary position of the local manager and his immediate subordinates as the personification of the banking group to existing and potential customers must be accepted. They are the bank, and national advertising will not wipe away shortcomings in local performance. In a situation, however, where the range and complexity of services provided by the bank and its associated companies is expanding rapidly, the ability of the branch manager to do full justice to his position is restricted. New solutions to this problem are needed which will undoubtedly encompass a considerable reduction in the administrative duties of the branch manager in favour of more direct profit-earning activities—a recognition that marketing skills have a much greater relative importance than was the case in times past.

(*c*) *Branch siting and styling*

Even in a small island like ours, people's tastes, needs and habits vary widely from area to area. There is no reason to feel that branch banking should necessarily be uniform. Buildings should be designed against a local backcloth, and indeed representation by the large banks is moving away from the commonly accepted forms of office towards premises which are designed and organized to meet local conditions. Moreover, the services provided should also be fitted to local demand. The requirements of the factory worker, the school teacher or the office employee contrast with that small number of customers with highly specialist needs—embracing taxation and the management of substantial investment portfolios—who may more appropriately be received in city offices of some splendour designed for their particular use.

The type of retail outlet for financial services which is brought to mind by the description 'money shop' undoubtedly has merits for handling the bulk of typical personal business. Such establishments are intended to be less expensive than the traditional branch in terms of type of premises used, the equipment involved and the security precautions required. The first moves in this direction, in the United Kingdom, have come from the secondary banks and finance houses, which have already moved a long way in establishing retail points of this nature.

Whatever system or systems eventually emerge from trial and error in the competition for the personal customer, certain features can be predicted:

(i) the premises will provide an open and attractive image rather than the secure but forbidding facade so reminiscent of our banking predecessors;

(ii) the siting of those parts of the building most regularly used by the individual customer will be convenient and immediately accessible to the most popular form of transport;

(iii) the services of the outlet will be provided, by one means or another, at a time convenient for most personal customers.

Within the office every form of labour-saving device will need to be exploited if a high standard of service in routine matters is to be provided for the personal customer at a reasonable price. Speed and excellence are, for example, required in payment transmission, the provision of cash and counter facilities and so on and the customer is entitled to expect that they will be available.

(d) The need to ensure simplicity in the routine relationship with the personal customer

Automation of routine operations has normally been introduced by commercial concerns to improve productivity; this is essentially true of banks. The requirements of the personal customer have been carefully considered and moulded to meet the constraints of the mechanical process.

While the customer is often willing to accept change, if it improves the reliability and availability of services, the innovation must retain a basic element of simplicity and straightforwardness.

(i) *Simpler charging policies for personal financial services.* It is, I think, a prerequisite of selling more financial services to a wider area of the population that the customer should know in advance what he will be required to pay. This is the age of precision in money matters, and in the context of personal business bankers are not going to be able to stand out as an exception.

The present price legislation in the United Kingdom reduces the opportunity for outright competition through the publication of tariffs by the commercial banks. Common charging schemes usually involve price adjustments which conflict in some instances with the Government's anti-inflation policies. Nevertheless, the major banks are already taking the initial steps in this direction.

(ii) *The provision of documentation relating to the bank account in a simple and easily readable form.* The statement of account should contain details of charges, enabling the customer to make an informed choice between competing banks and to maintain a regular check on the charge being levied.

(iii) *Easy to understand lending 'packages'*. Borrowing money for the first time is not an easy process for those not immediately involved with finance. A selection of lending services tailor-made for specific demands needs to be readily available and easily understood by the personal customer.

The economic administration of these 'off-the-shelf' schemes relies upon rapid decision-making, perhaps involving credit-scoring techniques where more credit information will be called for, particularly with new or little known customers. This situation would seem to call for the development of credit bureaux enjoying the support of the banking system and, by implication, required to maintain standards of competence, accuracy and ethical behaviour consistent with that relationship.

(iv) *Simple methods of completing banking business without visiting the branch.* In order to reduce the need for the customer to present himself at the bank—and also to reduce the growing pressure on premises—the banks will be trying to introduce more and more facilities which can be enjoyed at a distance. The use of cash dispensers, the postal application for a loan or revolving credit facility, the employment of mobile banks; all come into this category. Moreover, the possible expansion of automated payment systems into public buildings or even into individual homes—probably as an adjunct to the telephone system and made possible by the increasing acceptance of the credit card as a medium for settling debt—could persuade the ordinary citizen to reduce his reliance on cash. This approach to payment service could, of course, mean that a jointly owned enterprise might—on cost efficiency grounds—replace the present arrangement whereby each bank maintains a clearing system of its own.

(e) The place of the banker as personal adviser

Years of strict Government control on lending have increased the ordinary individual's view of the branch manager as a remote, negative figure in an environment designed primarily for the rich.

With more and more automation, and less need for the customer to visit the branch to conduct routine banking affairs, it is of especial importance that the manager and other counselling staff are readily available to provide advice and information in a friendly and unhurried atmosphere.

Of course the advice needs to be good, and delivered in the right way. While every effort can be made to make the branch attractive and convenient, in the end the customer will recall the manner and content of the interview. To this extent every customer does not always need to, or wish to, see the manager if his problem can be dealt with by junior staff in a manner which is competent and commands confidence. The important thing is that he should have a real sense of belonging.

(f) The contribution of staff recruitment, training and motivation

No progress can be made in improving personal services without the careful selection, training and motivation of branch staff. Some of the most important factors are as follows:

(i) *the acceptance that an individual's ability for salesmanship is as important as other technical qualifications.* Strong and attractive marketing methods will be employed to attract a customer and, once he is within the fold, to sell him as many services from the various elements of the banking group concerned as is possible.

This involves:

—more market research;

—well styled marketing and advertising;

—increased use of direct mail.

These will be wasted if insufficient time and skill are not available within the branch to exploit the success.

This implies:

—the need to continue sales training for those, like cashiers, who come into regular contact with customers;

—the continual review of training methods and content in relation to the practical needs at branch level;

—the encouragement of strong and effective inter-departmental and inter-company liaison within banking groups.

(ii) *the introduction of credible motivational and performance yardsticks designed to encourage and inform managers and staff.* The methods employed to judge individual effort or branch profit performance frequently fail to convince those they are meant to motivate—the branch staff. Simplicity and relevance are important. If these can be combined with yardsticks for justifying investment in new premises or for evaluating the profitability of particular services, so much the better, but their primary aim must be to measure the work of the branch and reward the staff concerned.

(iii) *the maintenance of traditional standards.* A new approach to staff training and a greater emphasis on increasing profit must not be allowed to depreciate the traditional values of security and reliability upon which the whole of the UK commercial banking reputation is based.

21. CONCLUSIONS

To attempt a summary is unnecessary and inappropriate but in the hope of being helpful perhaps I could say that my conclusions are these:

—there is considerable potential for gathering new accounts from an area of the population not presently in touch with the banks and also opportunities for selling further services to existing customers. Personal business will thus grow in significance in the affairs of commercial banking groups, both as an increasingly important contributor to deposits and as a growing source of revenue;

—a comprehensive financial service will increasingly be expected by the typical customer;

—the community will expect the banks to maintain a high standard of ethics in all their ventures, and marketing enthusiasm must not undermine this prime requirement;

—public opinion will presume the banks to be prominent in the general trend towards greater social responsibility in business affairs, and all developments will need to be measured against that yardstick. As an example, it will not be enough to provide consumer credit—it will be desirable also to help in widening the knowledge of the young citizen on personal financial matters as a contribution to society;

—both within the banking industry and outside its frontiers, there is increasing evidence of the desire for financial institutions to get involved in the money affairs of the private citizen. Competition in the whole area will thus increase, with new entrants encouraged by official measures of one sort and another. Profit margins are likely in consequence to be eroded in some departments of our business;

—the standing, strength and legal armoury of the consumer will grow;

—the position of the branch bank as a retail outlet through which more services are funnelled will become more and more apparent;

—the typical branch office for personal business will seek the maximum possible throughput of revenue-earning activity, offering certain services to non-customers on a single sale basis;

—banks will tend to provide more offices aimed particularly at the personal customer. Commercial accounts would then have their business relationship—though not necessarily their book-keeping—with larger branches much less widely available or even—in the the case of major customers—with regional centres having access to a full corporate finance capability;

—increasing use will be made of the credit card as a way of easing retail transactions by settling debt through on-line systems of widespread application. There is no doubt in my mind that this instrument will gradually gain greater significance in this field and will also grow in importance as the method of creating personal bank indebtedness;

—these developments must materially alter the pattern of recruitment and training of staff.

To those in banking everywhere this is a subject of substantial importance. It is also a social study of great fascination for much embraced therein is so closely interwoven in the fabric of the everyday life of the ordinary citizen. But this must be so, for banking is about people.

Financial Planning and Control

by Thomas I. Storrs

All of us involved in a profit-oriented organization have one ultimate measure of performance—and that is earnings. Earnings are not only an end in themselves but also the ultimate standard for all of us in judging how well we did our job of using scarce resources to provide products and services to the public—and also they are the standard for judging how well we managed our company in the process.

While almost everyone would agree that earnings are the best measure of management performance, the process of management is defined in various ways by different people. Diverse definitions, however, generally include the elements of planning and control as an integral part of the management process.

In my opinion, the presence of an effective financial planning and control system can in many cases make the difference between so-so results and outstanding performance. This assumes, of course, that the organization has the right kind of people to run the company.

The company of which I am president, N.C.N.B. Corporation, is a diversified bank holding company that has compiled over the past several years a record of which we are proud. Our compound growth rate of 22·4 % in earnings per share for the five years ended 1972 resulted in our being ranked number one on this count among the 50 largest banking organizations in the United States.

I believe our financial planning and control system has made a significant contribution to this performance. I should like to give you a brief description of this system and the manner in which it contributes to management effectiveness.

Overall planning and control, of course, include areas which are not directly financial, as well as short- and long-range or profit planning systems and related financial controls. These functions are a logical extension of our long-range planning efforts, which include the setting of strategic and directional goals and objectives.

Please understand that there is one thing I am *not* talking about. I have not used the word 'budgeting'. When many people think of financial planning, they think of budgeting. Budgeting is a passive, perhaps once-a-year, exercise in which large amounts of time or money are divided into smaller increments. This is but one step in the larger, continuous action-oriented planning and control process, and will be discussed in its proper place later on.

PLANNING IS CONTINUOUS

I indicated earlier that planning is a continuous process. To explain this, let me get somewhat theoretical for a moment and speak of planning in the abstract—without regard to whether we are managers in a bank, a bank holding company, or the A.B.C. Manufacturing Company.

When we manage, we are automatically planning, organizing, directing and controlling. The amount of time we spend on each item may vary, depending on our personal management styles, our placement within the organization, or the number of formal guidelines set up for us to follow.

And, as we go through these routines, we find that there are certain basic processes involved. Although we may not think of them consciously, they are there, and should be reviewed at this point:

1. *Perception.* This is planning in the total abstract. It is management day-dreaming. It is sitting back in your chair—or lying awake at night—and thinking about what you want your company to become in the future. Perception is the beginning of all planning.

2. *Analysis.* In the perception stage, you determine the direction in which your company is already travelling. In analysis, you try to figure out why by taking apart the various factors that are causing the move. And this in turn leads to

3. *Conceptual thought.* This is where the first element of control comes in. At this point, you begin to think of things you can cause to happen that will hopefully alter the course of events within your company. You are conceptualizing change.

4. *Communications and feedback.* Having thought of these ideas, you decide to communicate them to other people—and you want their opinions on whether and how they will work, or whether better options are available. This is communications and feedback.

5. *Decision.* Eventually, and if for no other reason than that the future has suddenly become the present, you must choose among the ideas that have been developed.

6. *Action.* This is the point at which you must assign resources —manpower, time, money—whatever is necessary to convert your ideas into action. This often is the most difficult step in the planning process, because this is the place where those thoughts that looked perfectly beautiful on paper sometimes don't work out so well in practice.

7. *Monitoring and Control.* Having gotten something in motion, you don't just let it go. You build in a system for guidance and correction. The recent trips to the moon represented the almost-ultimate in planning and control—and you will remember that optional mid-course corrections were a vital part of the process.

Although we have been speaking of planning in the abstract, I think it wise to mention a couple of concrete points here. Abstract does not mean subjective or theoretical. The entire planning process must take place on an objective, real-world basis.

Before we make decisions concerning the future, we must evaluate conditions affecting our present. We must be aware of our company's limitations and capabilities—and, at the same time, we must do some forecasting about what our competition probably will plan and do. Equally important is an analysis and projection of economic, social and governmental forces that might be involved.

It would make little sense, for example, to set a goal of a given increase in time deposits in a given period, when we know that the competition and the economy will not permit us to do this. This is where objectivity must take precedence over enthusiasm.

The planning process I have just described obviously takes considerable time. We also can become so involved and so expert in planning that we come up with dozens and dozens of schemes leading to a brighter future. Obviously, a few or several of these schemes should take priority. And here is where a vitally critical part of planning comes into play: setting priorities, or planning our plans.

BUT WHY BOTHER?

Any detailed planning process obviously takes considerable time—and, when extended to a corporate-wide basis, considerable money. This forces, then, the logical question: Why bother? Why have a financial planning system, particularly if your company is already a profitable one?

This question can be answered in three parts:

First, the corporation that approaches the planning process in the way I have described will discover that the way it assigns priorities produces a corporate direction. A company's managers may want growth in size or geography. They may want additional profits, to be known as the friendliest institution in town, the most efficient, the largest, or whatever the case may be . . . and these goals will automatically be spelled out as the planning process is carried out.

Another output is that year-long guidelines for achieving corporate policies and goals will be established—as will short-run tactics or work plans. Finally, we will end up with a month-by-month roadmap for utilizing the basic resources of our company in achieving goals and implementing corporate philosophies.

PLANNING DISCIPLINES

Before leaving the general subject of planning, I should emphasize one crucial point: planning must be developed from the grass roots up. Although guidance may be provided by top management, each management level in a company must participate if the ultimate plan is to be universally accepted and realistic in achievement potential.

Admittedly, there must be an established structure and a central focal point to coordinate and oversee the planning process—but the function of this focal point is to guide, not to do the actual planning.

You may have observed that to this point I have said nothing about numbers—dollars, percentages or whatever. This is because profit planning is the financial expression of goals and of the assignment of resources to achieve them. It is only after we have determined what our ends are and what resources are available to us that we can begin to put numbers on paper.

It is important that continuity be built in—that we do not stop once we have a profit plan set up for a given period. We need to be constantly aware of whether we are achieving our goals, so that we may make the necessary adjustments if we are going off course.

And this is where numbers and reports begin to play a greater role. The results of our day-to-day activities are shown in various reports, financial and otherwise. It is important that procedures be established to compare these results to our plan. This is the control method that is so crucial to the overall planning programme—and the establishment of this control also gives all employees a constant reminder that they are working under a concerted plan and not free-lancing. As I stated earlier, the establishment of a continuous planning process helps us all to be better managers on a daily basis.

SOUNDS GOOD—BUT DOES IT WORK?

One can espouse theory forever, but the inevitable question arises: 'Does it work?' Perhaps the best way to seek an answer to this question where planning and control are involved is to see if any corporation is doing it successfully—and what results are being achieved.

I apologize for using N.C.N.B. Corporation as my model for proper financial planning and control, but I do so for two reasons. The first is that, as president of N.C.N.B. Corporation, I know something about the company and can share with you our practical experiences. Second, a number of financial analysts and other people who should know have told me that we have the best financial planning and control programme of any banking company in the United States. This statement may or may not be true. More important for our present purposes is my conviction that our system has made a significant contribution to the performance of our company as measured at the bottom of the profit-and-loss statement.

WHAT IS THE 'RIGHT' PLANNING PROGRAMME?

A very real problem exists in describing a case study of a particular organization. Sometimes the reader gets the impression that the methods described are the only ones that can be used. Please do not infer this from my comments. The 'right' financial planning and control programme is whatever is right for a particular organization. As a major financial company with 10 subsidiaries and more than 250 offices, it is necessary that we use a sophisticated, computerized programme. The same may not be true for your company. Effective planning and control systems do not have to be fancy and, as I describe the programme at N.C.N.B. Corporation, I hope that the underlying concepts, involvement of management, control features and effectiveness of the programme take precedence in your mind over the specifics of the system.

Nor would I have you think that we have always performed satisfactorily in financial planning. As a matter of fact, we made some attempts several years ago which did not follow the concepts I mentioned earlier. Planning in this instance was essentially balance-sheet planning and was done in the central office. In retrospect, it looks very primitive and only moderately effective, but it whetted our appetite for the system we now have.

Early in 1967, we initiated a programme in the bank's control department to begin a thorough planning and control procedure involving both balance-sheet and profit-and-loss items. We discovered quickly that few people in banking believed such a system was completely applicable to our industry—so we had to reach into other industries to find people who had been doing this sort of thing for many years—and who had not learned that it wasn't feasible in banking!

PLANNING NEXT YEAR'S PROFITS

Let me get down to the specifics of our programme, which has undergone many refinements since our 1967 beginning.

We might begin by saying that the beginning of next year's profit plan starts with a constant monitoring of the current year's plan. During each year, we periodically monitor our activities and project them to the end of the year via an earnings simulation model. At several key points during the year, we feed into this computerized model various assumptions of prime rate changes, money costs, economic factors and other forces that have real or potential effect on earnings. These are matched with our operating results to date—and a projection of current-year earnings is obtained. The answers are reviewed closely by management, giving particular attention to the underlying determinants as well as the results.

In September, a projection of the next year is prepared. This projection, going beyond the simulation model input, essentially is an extension into the next year of the company's operations against the expected economic environment. The initial computation is called the staff projection and reflects the technical views of 25 to 30 of our best-qualified managers and staff executives. Senior management tests the results against its judgments and plans, and the revised management plan becomes the base upon which planning for the next year takes form.

During this same period, we are taking a look at current-year capital expenditures and beginning to project them—into the following year and the next four years after that.

Upon completion of the management plan, which in effect sets goals for the coming year, and the capital expenditure plan, which gives an indication of the resources necessary to fund our growth in fixed assets, overall earnings goals and other guidelines are established for the next year. This management decision provides top-level guidance for the upcoming profit plan. In calling this management's decision, I would stress that top management does the deciding only after much consultation with middle and lower management. The heads of each major unit of the company consult with their managers in determining what they believe to be realistic goals and guidelines. As many meetings as necessary are held to ensure the setting of proper priorities and goals—and our earnings simulation model is used time and again.

During the months of October and November, our 1,000 first-line supervisors compile a first draft of the profit plans for their units—the sum of which will represent the corporate profit plan. (I might point out here that out of a total staff of 4,000 persons, 1,000 are responsible for primary plan development; with these 1,000 consulting their own staff in turn, we have a large measure of participation in profit planning.) Each manager and loan officer projects, where applicable, his loan levels, deposit levels, loan yields, deposit rates, headcount and expense items. Each then comes up with a month-by-month income and expense projection for his area of responsibility.

The plans of the various managers are summarized and the results analysed during November and December. Comparisons with the guidelines and the total management plan are constantly made, and differences explained or adjusted—or both. Where changes are appropriate, they are submitted *by the managers of the primary units*.

If it appears during the course of the analysis that a particular guideline or objective is impossible to achieve, the figures are adjusted accordingly. By the same token, we request adjustments upward when it is apparent that unit plans may be lacking somewhat in ambition. In late December, after all appropriate adjustments have been made, the profit plan is submitted to senior management for approval.

Approval of the plan is one of the major items on the agenda of our January board of directors' meeting. The plan is explained to the board by a senior executive. He presents our goals and objectives for the coming year and compares them to the prior year's performance. I can assure you that this is not a perfunctory presentation. Board members are actively interested and indicate their approval or disapproval of the projected results and the assumptions and plans underlying them.

We do not leave the plan idle after board approval. Each month, a comparison of actual performance versus planned performance is made for each primary unit and various summary levels—all the way to top management. These reports are prepared in our Control Department, and they are used by every manager within the company. Each month finds these managers changing work plans and other objectives in order to achieve the profit plan—although the profit plan itself is not changed during the course of a year.

A SAMPLE REPORTING SYSTEM

Results are reported and replanning is done at N.C.N.B. through the use of several types of reports, each of which is geared to the different segments of management and each of which covers different items. The total package presents a comprehensive view of that ultimate measure: *earnings*. Let me list the types of reports we use, after which we can look at some samples.

The *Responsibility Report*, which displays current-month actual figures, year-to-date actual figures and variance from plan in each category, is distributed to each primary unit—to each of the 1,000 units which prepare a profit plan. *Summary Responsibility Reports*, which are distributed to various higher levels of management, will be discussed later.

Profit Centre Reporting is a means to measure the contribution of specific organizations to the overall profitability of N.C.N.B. Corporation, while *Key Item Reports* present various statistical items that are not necessarily financial in terms of dollars and cents but which are an integral part in the monitoring of overall performance.

Management control reports are prepared monthly, and in them financial information is presented in a narrative form to senior management. *Product profitability reporting* is another name for functional costing analysis. When combined with profit-centre reporting, product profitability reporting permits management to know not only which organizations, but also which product lines, are contributing to earnings gains or deficits.

Work measurement reports are extremely important, since personnel expense is the largest single non-interest expense

Dear Barry,
We are on
our annual leave now,
touring the Far East. We
have been to Bangkok,
Chong Mai, Hong Kong, Taipei,
and the mountains of Taiwan.
We are now in Manila, and
tonight we fly to Sydney.
The last five days will be spent
on Kuta beach in Bali. Then back
to Singapore for a rest. Yours,

A beautiful Philippine scenery
with coconut palms, seashore and hills.

Geof, Rae, Marcus, Daniel and Matthew.

National
NATIONAL BOOK STORE
MANILA, PHILIPPINES

DISTRIBUTED BY NATIONAL BOOK STORE, MANILA PHILIPPINES

KRUGER 37448

Mr B. Melbourne-Webb,
FNCA/112, Internal Audit,
SHELL INTERNATIONAL
PETROLEUM CO.
SHELL CENTRE,
LONDON SE1, UK.

category in a bank. Finally, *special financial analyses* are prepared when events deem it necessary.

RESPONSIBILITY REPORTING

Since responsibility reporting is the keystone of our system, I propose to discuss the contents of these reports in detail. Responsibility reports bring the concepts of planning and control closer together than any other system, and also receive the widest distribution. The reports are designed to improve our ability to control the operating earnings of N.C.N.B. Corporation—and contain certain built-in concepts which we believe make them successful in their task.

First, reporting of income and expense follows the organizational structure. In other words, our financial reporting system and our management decision-making structure follow the same organizational lines.

Second, each unit is held responsible only for those items it can control. For instance, our proof operations are centralized in three regional processing centres. Although each is physically located in a city where the bank has a retail office, the cost of processing items is not controllable by that city office. So the centres, and not the city offices, prepare a plan for this expense and are held accountable.

As I mentioned earlier, the plan is not changed during the year once it has been approved. This may sound somewhat contradictory to some of my earlier points about replanning—but replanning should involve adjusting work plans and day-to-day activities to your goals rather than changing your goals. We do not shoot at a moving target.

Third, variances from plan are determined at the lowest level and 'pyramided', thus enabling management to determine responsibility at each succeeding level and take action to ensure that plan objectives are achieved. If each level of management takes action to adjust the proper portion of the plan, then the total organization will achieve its goals.

NCNB CORPORATION **EXHIBIT A**

RESPONSIBILITY REPORT

1000-7750-7700-0000 PRIMARY REPORT FEBRUARY, 1973

MIDDLEVILLE

Current month Actual	Current month Variance		Description	Year to date Actual	Year to date Variance	Annual profit plan
		INCOME				
1	1	44200	COMMERCIAL CHECK	1	1	
	–	44500	SAVINGS	1	1	
1	1	TOT	DEPOSIT FEES	2	2	
12	1–	45100	FEE OFFICIAL CK	27	–	168
29	20	45300	HANDLING CHARGES	35	17	108
41	18	TOT	GENERAL BANK FEE	63	17	276
9	6–	49100	SAF DEP BOX RENT	18	12–	180
9	6–	TOT	OTHER INCOME	18	12–	180
52	14		DIRECT INCOME	83	7	456
	37.5		PERCENT VARIANCE		10.0	
		EXPENSE				
2,022	77	52100	REG SAL—WAGES	3,905	244	25,150
	10	52200	OVERTIME		20	120
303	13	52300	FRINGE BENE DIST	585	40	3,796
2,325	101	TOT	PERSONNEL EXP	4,491	304	29,066
325	325–	53100	RENT	650	650–	
162	162–	53300	DEPR AND AMORT	330	330–	
487	487–	TOT	OCCUPANCY EXP	980	980–	
2	2–	54200	PUBLIC RELATIONS	5	5–	
	10	54300	BUS DEVELOPMENT		20	120
2	7	TOT	MARKETING EXP	5	15	120
71	495	55200	DEPRECIATION	167	966	6,804
220	194–	TOT	MAINT AND REPAIR	220	159–	321
291	301	TOT	EQUIPMENT EXP	388	806	7,125
1	3	57300	STAT AND SUPP	1	8	60
69	6–	57400	TELEPHONE AND WIRE	138	12–	756
	5	57800	MISC OPER EXP	2–	12	60
48	38–	57900	CLERICAL ERRORS	55	35–	120
119	36–	TOT	GEN OPER EXP	193	27–	996
32	7–	58300	ADM TRAV AND ENT	52	2–	294
32	7–	TOT	GEN ADM EXPENSES	52	2–	294
3,259	121–		DIRECT EXPENSE	6,111	115	37,601
	3.9–		PERCENT VARIANCE		1.9	

–Indicates unfavourable variance.

(All names used in exhibits are illustrative.)

The best way to explain a responsibility report is to look at one. The first items to catch your attention probably are the two shaded columns. These columns are highlighted purposely because they represent the variance from plan—and since plan is what we are trying to achieve, the amount of the variance is of critical importance. A dash to the right of the number indicates an unfavourable variance: income below plan, or expense above plan. We do not confine our examination of variances to the unfavourable ones. A significant favourable variance may indicate good performance—or an improper planning job. If anticipated earnings are understated, for example, this poor planning may lead to a poor corporate decision. This could be as dangerous as overstating earnings. As I mentioned earlier, we seek a realistic plan, one that is neither too difficult to achieve nor too easy to achieve.

Total dollar variances mean different things, depending on the size of the unit involved. It is for this reason that we show the percent variance as well as the dollar variance. You will note that both monthly and year-to-date figures are included. The plan for the total year is shown in the right-hand column as a reference point. The monthly plan is not shown, since the important monthly items are the actual results and where and why they have varied from the plan.

To aid the first-line supervisor in determining his variances from the plan, a Transaction and Balance Journal is prepared that details each transaction made affecting his unit. Thus the manager has at his disposal, on a monthly basis, his previously prepared plans, his variance from same, and detailed information which permits him to replan and adjust to achieve his goals.

As president, I cannot sit down and study each of 1,000 primary reports. Instead, I receive a number of summary reports. A key point in our system is to present to each succeeding level of management only that amount of detail necessary for informed decision-making.

When an executive up the ladder from the primary unit

NCNB CORPORATION EXHIBIT B
TRANSACTION AND BALANCE JOURNAL

30-77-777 1000-7750-7700-0000 FRIENDLY BRANCH FEBRUARY, 1973

	Transaction Detail			Amounts	
Account Number	Date	Entry ref.	Description	Current month	Year to date
	00/00/00	P–0000000	PAYROLL	7.07	
	00/00/00	P–0000000	PAYROLL	139.62	
	00/00/00	P–0000000	PAYROLL	10.44	
	00/00/00	P–0000000	PAYROLL	126.50	
	00/00/00	P–0000000	PAYROLL	8.16	
	00/00/00	P–0000000	PAYROLL	3.26	
52,300			FRINGE BENE DIST	303.32	585.91
52,000			PERSONNEL EXP	2,325.44	4,491.86
		V–131047	INTERSTATE DE	325.00	
53,100			RENT	325.00	650.00
	00/00/00	F–0000000	DEPRECIATION EXP	143.12	
53,310			D–A PREMISES	143.12	291.96
	00/00/00	F–0000000	DEPRECIATION EXP	19.33	
53,340			D–A BLDG EQUIP	19.33	38.66
53,300			DEPR AND AMORT	162.45	330.62
53,000			OCCUPANCY EXP	487.45	980.62
	00/00/00	T–0000000	DR/CR TICKET	2.35	
54,240			PR CUST PARKING	2.35	5.00
54,200			PUBLIC RELATIONS	2.35	5.00
54,000			MARKETING EXP	2.35	5.00
	00/00/00	F–0000000	DEPRECIATION EXP	20.31	
55,210			DEPR FURN AND FIX	20.31	40.62
	00/00/00		DEPRECIATION EXP	51.20	
55,220			DEPR MACH-EQUIP	51.20	127.36
55,200			DEPRECIATION	71.51	167.98
		V–217238	1 BUS MACHINE	72.00	
		V–217185	1 BURROUGHS	148.43	
55,320			CONT-MAINT-OTHER	220.43	220.43
55,300			MAINT AND REPAIR	220.43	220.43
55,000			EQUIPMENT EXP	291.94	338.41
		V–217241	1 BRADY PRINT	1.75	
57,390			S-S OTHER	1.75	1.75
57,300			STAT AND SUPP	1.75	1.75
		V–217239	1 SOUTHERN BELL	69.25	
57,410			TEL L/S EQUIP	69.25	138.54

NCNB CORPORATION **EXHIBIT C**

RESPONSIBILITY REPORT

1000-7750-0000-0000 FEBRUARY, 1973

PYRAMID REPORT—SUMMARY BY UNIT

MIDDLEVILLE

Current month Actual	Current month Variance	Description	Year to date Actual	Year to date Variance	Annual profit plan
		INCOME			
54,993	593–	COM LOAN AND MKTG	114,224	1,585	659,525
9,063	352	OPERATIONS	19,282	1,845	108,232
109,612	15	CONSUMER CREDIT	226,907	8,641	1,365,091
1,305	327–	BANKING HOUSES	2,915	350–	19,596
174,975	552–	TOTAL INCOME	363,329	11,721	2,152,444
		EXPENSE			
9,150	369–	CITY EXEC ADMIN	17,823	653	121,701
8,483	456–	COM LOAN AND MKTG	17,662	1,204–	96,023
126,590	7,903–	OPERATIONS	252,805	12,394–	1,541,128
12,183	3,049–	CONSUMER CREDIT	22,949	4,709–	119,008
6,938	284–	BANKING HOUSES	12,813	321	85,935
163,346	12,063–	TOTAL EXPENSE	324,054	17,333–	1,963,795

–Indicates unfavourable variance.

wishes additional detail, he goes back through his organizational chain of command to the departmental manager or supervisor concerned and asks him to explain any variances. In this manner we tie both the planning process and control and follow-up to the total organization.

All monthly responsibility reports and transaction and balance journals are prepared by the third working day of the following month. This timeliness permits immediate follow-up and correction, so that the following month's report hopefully will show better results. All of the components in our financial planning and control system, in fact, have timeliness as an important underlying concept. I will indicate appropriate timetables in discussing our other reports—but I am sure you will notice that in all cases they are produced with considerable speed.

You might say that a responsibility report represents the books of the corporation:

NCNB CORPORATION **EXHIBIT D**
RESPONSIBILITY REPORT

1000-7750-0000-0000 FEBRUARY, 1973

PYRAMID REPORT—INCOME AND EXPENSE BY UNIT

MIDDLEVILLE

Current month Actual	Current month Variance	Description	Year to date Actual	Year to date Variance	Annual profit plan
		CONSOLIDATED INCOME			
140,027	3,359–	INT LOAN-DISC	286,886	604–	1,753,032
24,644	2,847	LOAN FEES	54,294	10,880	271,584
7,326	103–	DEPOSIT FEES	16,208	1,348	92,760
579	171	GENERAL BANK FEE	872	56	4,956
67–	67–	SERVICE EARNING	102–	102–	
2,465	40–	OTHER INCOME	5,169	142	30,112
174,975	552–	TOTAL INCOME	363,329	11,721	2,152,444
	0.3–	PERCENT VARIANCE		3.3	
		EXPENSE			
99,150	6,083–	INTEREST EXPENSE	202,373	12,873–	1,232,609
43,506	2,078–	PERSONNEL EXP	85,096	2,693–	512,270
4,049	562–	OCCUPANCY EXP	8,086	1,112–	47,777
1,412	49	MARKETING EXP	4,287	645–	22,612
5,865	2,478–	EQUIPMENT EXP	7,937	1,764–	33,962
904	64–	PROF FEE AN SERV	1,072	1,732	22,830
7,494	738–	GEN OPER EXP	12,634	877	81,069
917	61–	GEN ADM EXPENSES	1,790	78–	10,666
45	45–	CREDIT/COLL EXP	775	775–	
163,346	12,063–	TOTAL EXPENSE	324,054	17,333–	1,963,795
	8.0–	PERCENT VARIANCE		5.7–	

–Indicates unfavourable variance.

The SUM of *Income* and *Expenses* as shown on Responsibility Reports

EQUALS *Income* and *Expenses* of each subsidiary

and finally

The *Income Before Securities Gains and Losses*

of the total corporation.

Effective use of the responsibility reporting system, then, gives us early insight in determining what our earnings are and in making timely mid-course changes.

NCNB CORPORATION RESPONSIBILITY REPORT — EXHIBIT E

1000-7750-0000-0000 FEBRUARY, 1973

CONSOLIDATED INCOME AND EXPENSE
MIDDLEVILLE

Current month Actual	Current month Variance	Description	Year to date Actual	Year to date Variance	Annual profit plan
		CONSOLIDATED INCOME			
17,353	490	42110 COMR LN TIME	37,622	2,214	166,414
895	360	42120 COMR LN DEMAND	2,531	1,403	7,100
8,760	1,050–	42130 COMR LN TERM	17,290	2,215–	128,932
27,008	200–	TOT COMM LOANS	57,444	1,402	302,446
38,609	3,418–	42270 DIRECT LOANS	77,171	6,472–	526,344
41,222	370	42280 INDIRECT LOANS	85,541	4,173	508,123
79,832	3,047–	TOT CONSUMER CDT	162,713	2,298–	1,034,467
5,959	40–	42300 FLOOR PLAN LNS	12,506	506	72,000
18,922	1,811	42630 MORT LN CONV RES	37,494	3,466	215,646
6,918	2,041–	42640 MORT LN CONV COM	13,856	3,966–	112,479
25,841	229–	TOT MORTGAGE LOANS	51,350	500–	328,125
1,385	158	42700 CONSTRUCTION LN	2,871	285	15,994
140,027	3,359–	TOT INT LOAN-DISC	286,886	604–	1,753,032
18	18	43160 ALL OTHER FEES	43	43	
18	18	TOT COMM LOANS	43	43	
902	10,427–	43250 DIRECT LOANS	20,877	1,672–	141,900
22,491	13,271	43260 INDIRECT LOANS	30,050	11,680	114,720
23,394	2,844	TOT TIME PAYMENT LN	50,927	10,007	256,620
426	259	43300 FLOOR PLAN LNS	759	425	2,004
804	95–	43600 MORT LN FEES	2,228	428	10,800
	180–	43700 CONSTRUCTION LN	335	25–	2,160
24,644	2,847	TOT LOAN FEES	54,294	10,880	271,584
5,366	233–	44100 INDIVIDUAL CK	12,571	1,371	69,000
1,946	146	44200 COMMERCIAL CK	3,572	27–	23,400
13	16–	44500 SAVINGS	64	4	360
7,326	103–	TOT DEPOSIT FEES	16,208	1,348	92,760
100	2	45100 FEE OFFICIAL CK	194	1–	1,176
478	168	45300 HANDLING CHGS	678	58	3,780
579	171	TOT GENERAL BK FEE	872	56	4,956
67–	67–	46200 DATA PCESS FEE	102–	102–	
67–	67–	TOT SERVICE EARNING	102–	102–	
1,150	287	49100 SAF DEP BOX RNT	2,244	503	10,396
1,305	327–	49700 RENTAL INCOME	2,915	350–	19,596
9	–	49900 OTHER INCOME	6	10–	120
2,465	40–	TOT OTHER INCOME	5,169	142	30,112
174,975	552–	DIRECT INCOME	363,329	11,721	2,152,444
	0.3–	PERCENT VARIANCE		3.3	

–Indicates unfavourable variance.

MEASURING ORGANIZATIONS

Additional insight beyond that shown on responsibility reports is helpful in determining why we earned what we did in a given period. This leads to other programmes—specifically profit-centre reporting, which permits a measurement of the contribution to earnings by given organizational units.

Not every unit is or should be a profit centre. As is the case with most financial planning and control systems, the definition of a profit centre is whatever we wish it to be. At N.C.N.B., the primary purpose of defining a profit centre is to enable us to look at each income-producing unit as though it were a separate entity.

Support units which may be regionalized or centralized, such as marketing, communications, personnel, operations centres and the like, are not considered profit centres. However, since the purpose of the 'non-profit centres' is to serve the profit centres, their expenses and income need to be distributed in an equitable fashion to the profit centres.

In addition, our investment portfolio is centralized at N.C.N.B. Its funding comes primarily from those profit centres having excess deposits. Thus the earnings of the investment portfolio rightfully belong to the profit centres and are so reallocated, again on an equitable basis.

If one keeps in mind that the purpose of setting up profit centres is to gain additional insight into the manner in which we achieve our income before securities gains and losses, it follows that the sum of the income of all profit centres must equal the sum of all income as shown on the responsibility reports:

Direct Earnings of all profit centres PLUS
Investment Income, LESS
The *Net Direct Expenses* of the non-profit centres
EQUALS
Income Before Securities Gains or Losses

Although the concept is simple, it is important that various

EXHIBIT F

NORTH CAROLINA NATIONAL BANK
A SUBSIDIARY OF NCNB CORPORATION
PROFIT CENTRE REPORT

MIDDLEVILLE FEBRUARY, 1973

(Dollar amounts in thousands)

Current month Actual	Current month Variance		Year-to-date Actual	Year-to-date Variance
$	$		$	$
140.0	3.4–	INTEREST ON LOANS	286.9	0.6–
24.7	2.8	LOAN FEES	54.3	10.9
7.3	0.1–	DEPOSIT FEES	16.2	1.3
3.0	0.1	OTHER INCOME	5.9	0.1
175.0	0.6–	DIRECT INCOME	363.3	11.7
99.2	6.1–	INTEREST EXPENSE	202.4	12.9–
43.5	2.1–	PERSONNEL EXPENSE	85.1	2.7–
4.0	0.6–	OCCUPANCY EXPENSE	8.1	1.1–
5.9	2.5–	EQUIPMENT EXPENSE	8.0	1.7–
5.4	0.7–	GENERAL OPERATING EXPENSE	8.5	0.9
0.9	0.1–	GENERAL ADMINISTRATIVE EXPENSE	1.8	0.1–
2.1	– –	PROVISION FOR LOAN LOSSES	4.1	– –
2.3	– –	OTHER EXPENSE	6.1	0.3
163.3	12.1–	DIRECT EXPENSE	324.1	17.3–
11.7	12.7–	DIRECT EARNINGS	39.2	5.6–
58.1	1.8–	INTRA-BANK INTEREST	117.9	1.1–
69.8	14.5–	CONTROLLABLE EARNINGS	157.1	6.7–
14.0		OPERATIONS CENTRE	28.8	
1.9		ADVERTISING	3.8	
1.9		INSURANCE	3.8	
3.9		PERSONNEL	7.8	
4.3		LOAN AND DEPOSIT SERVICES	8.6	
1.1		OTHER SERVICES	2.1	
- –		SERVICES PURCHASED FROM PROFIT CENTRES	– –	
– –		SERVICES SOLD TO PROFIT CENTRES	– –	
27.1		SERVICES PURCHASED (NET)	54.9	
42.7	14.5–	CONTRIBUTION TO PROFIT BEFORE INDIRECT EARNINGS AND CHARGES	102.2	6.7–
32.6		EARNINGS FROM EMPLOYED CAPITAL	68.8	
13.3		INDIRECT CHARGES	21.8	
62.0	14.5–	INCOME BEFORE TAXES AND SECURITIES—GAINS/LOSSES	149.2	6.7–
31.7	7.4	APPLICABLE INCOME TAXES	76.3	3.5
30.3	7.1–	INCOME BEFORE SECURITIES GAINS/LOSSES	72.9	3.2–
37.7		EARNINGS REQUIRED FOR 13% RETURN ON EMPLOYED CAPITAL	77.2	
3,483		EMPLOYED CAPITAL	3,561	
10.4		RETURN ON EMPLOYED CAPITAL (%)	12.3	

—Indicates unfavourable effect on earnings.

distributions be made equitably. It is the job of our control department to ensure that this occurs.

We have been able to do this by developing an extremely effective system of standard costing based on extensive work measurement and other techniques. This permits us not only to determine the full cost of services, but also to determine direct, indirect, fixed, variable, overhead and similar costs that might not always be immediately apparent.

A full discussion of the technical aspects of these calculations would require hours and days—but since the purpose of this paper and of our reports is to aid people in managing, perhaps we could spend our time more fruitfully by looking at a profit-centre report and discussing its use to management.

As you can see, considerable information is contained in a profit-centre report. Direct income and expenses, both monthly and for the year to date, are taken from the summary responsibility report of the profit centre in question. The difference between the two obviously represents direct earnings—and the variance shows quickly whether earnings goals were met or missed and by how much.

I mentioned earlier that our profit planning includes both balance sheet and profit-and-loss items. The funds position of a particular profit centre, whether it be a funds provider or a user, is reflected in the intra-bank interest figures shown immediately after direct earnings. Intra-bank interest is the name we give our pricing of funds transfers. Again, without attempting to get into the specifics of intra-bank interest calculations, we price our funds transfers at the marginal or incremental funds rate. In other words, if the profit centre were an independent bank, the rate of intra-bank interest expense or income would approximate to what that independent bank would have received or paid in a short-term money market.

Direct Earnings, PLUS OR MINUS *Intra-bank Interest*,

EQUAL

The *Controllable Earnings* of the profit centre.

The several categories following controllable earnings are collectively what we call 'services purchased'. These are the services that the profit centres buy from the various support units within the bank. You will note that no variances are shown for these items. This is because the profit centres are charged at a standard cost, and the expense varies strictly with volume.

The 'earnings from employed capital and indirect charges' category represents essentially overhead income and overhead expense. Since the sum of income from all profit centres must equal total income before securities gains or losses, these items must be counted. The presentation of our profit centre report, however, makes it possible for the profit centre manager and anyone else to determine the amount due to factors beyond the control of the profit centre.

The calculation of taxes permits the determination for the profit centres of income before securities gains and losses—as well as variance from plan, both on a monthly and year-to-date basis. The sum of all profit centres equals income before securities gains or losses.

As part of the planning process each year, we determine the return on employed capital that we should attain. As a further measurement of a profit centre, we determine monthly whether that centre is achieving this return regardless of absolute earnings or variances from plan. Capital is assigned to a profit centre based on its loans and deposits, and a monthly and year-to-date return is determined.

Since profit and loss items were not the only ones included in the plan, actual and plan levels (both current month and year-to-date) are shown for all balance sheet categories. Yields on assets and rates on sources of funds are similarly depicted. Data on the number of accounts, the number of people, the number of deposits, etc., are all included as part of the monthly reporting cycle.

The profit centre report provides a complete picture of what

EXHIBIT G

NORTH CAROLINA NATIONAL BANK
A SUBSIDIARY OF NCNB CORPORATION
KEY ITEM REPORT

MIDDLEVILLE FEBRUARY, 1973

Average Levels (In $ Millions) Current Month Actual	Current Month Plan	Year to Date Actual	Year to Date Plan		Rates and Yields (%) Current Month Actual	Current Month Plan	Year to Date Actual	Year to Date Plan
				AVERAGE DEPOSITS				
				DEMAND DEPOSITS				
0.4	0.5	0.4	0.6	T.T. AND LOAN				
4.7	4.7	4.6	4.7	INDIVIDUAL				
9.0	8.6	9.3	8.8	COMMERCIAL				
0.7	1.3	1.0	1.0	PUBLIC FUNDS				
0.7	0.7	0.7	0.7	OTHER				
15.5	15.8	16.0	15.8	TOTAL DEMAND				
				TIME DEPOSITS				
12.3	12.8	12.2	12.6	SAVINGS DEPOSITS	4.48	4.50	4.49	4.50
2.6	2.5	2.6	2.5	BONUS SAVINGS	4.90	5.01	4.95	5.01
6.9	6.4	6.8	6.4	NCNB CTFS.	5.28	5.29	5.28	5.30
3.6	1.6	3.5	1.6	NEGOTIABLE C/D'S	4.95	5.82	5.16	5.82
0.3	0.5	0.3	0.5	PUBLIC FUNDS	4.26	4.91	4.26	4.91
--	--	--	--	OTHER	--	--	--	--
25.7	23.8	25.4	23.6	TOTAL TIME	4.80	4.87	4.84	4.87
41.2	39.6	41.4	39.4	TOTAL DEPOSITS				
				AVERAGE LOANS				
5.2	4.7	5.3	4.7	COMMERCIAL LOANS	6.65	7.33	6.61	7.32
12.4	11.3	12.2	11.2	CONSUMER CREDIT LOANS	12.58	13.26	13.20	13.26
1.0	1.0	1.0	1.0	FLOOR PLAN LOANS	7.70	7.78	7.81	7.52
4.5	4.3	4.5	4.3	MORTGAGE LOANS	7.12	7.55	7.21	7.55
0.2	0.2	0.2	0.2	CONSTRUCTION LOANS	7.76	8.88	8.65	8.99
0.2	--	0.2	--	OTHER LOANS	--	--	--	--
23.5	21.5	23.4	21.4	TOTAL LOANS	8.52	9.33	8.79	9.32

	Percentage Deposit and Loan Growth: This month last month this year	compared to this month last year	This year to date compared to last year to date
DEMAND DEPOSITS	6.6–	8.4	13.5
TIME DEPOSITS	2.4	24.8	23.3
TOTAL DEPOSITS	1.2–	18.1	19.3
COMMERCIAL LOANS	5.5–	26.8	32.5
CONSUMER CREDIT LOANS[1]	3.3	51.2	48.8
TOTAL LOANS	0.9	42.4	43.6

Past due Loans ($000)	5–30 Days	Over 30 Days	30–60 Days	Over 60 Days
COMMERCIAL[2]	11.8	2.5		
CONSTRUCTION[2]	– –	– –		
CONSUMER CREDIT[3]			1.6	2.0
MORTGAGE[2]			– –	– –

	Current Month		Year to Date	
Charge-Offs ($000)	Actual	Year ago	Actual	Year ago
CHARGE-OFFS	4.1	2.3	7.3	4.4
RECOVERIES	0.5	0.4	4.1	0.5
NET	3.6–	1.9–	3.2–	3.9–

1 Yield on cash employed basis.
2 Balance of loan.
3 Overdue payment.

happened in a given profit centre during the previous month and for the year to date. In order to make this reporting useful, each profit centre manager makes monthly comments and lists steps that he is taking in the replanning process.

EXHIBIT H

NORTH CAROLINA NATIONAL BANK
A SUBSIDIARY OF NCNB CORPORATION
STATISTICAL SUMMARY

MIDDLEVILLE FEBRUARY, 1973

General statistics

	Feb., 1973	Jan., 1973	Feb., 1972
LOANS:	$	$	$
COMMERCIAL	5,147	5,447	4,064
CONSUMER CREDIT	13,442	13,035	9,123
MORTGAGE	4,488	4,430	3,093
CONSTRUCTION	231	221	166
TOTAL LOANS	23,451	23,306	16,463
DEPOSITS:			
INDIVIDUAL DEMAND	4,677	4,615	4,050
COMMERCIAL DEMAND	8,950	9,655	8,186
OTHER DEMAND	1,839	2,356	2,113
TOTAL DEMAND	15,466	16,626	14,349
SAVINGS DEPOSITS	12,285	12,159	10,340
NEGOTIABLE C/D'S	3,557	3,535	1,762
PUBLIC FUNDS	250	250	49
OTHER TIME	9,561	9,210	8,481
TOTAL TIME	25,653	25,154	20,632
TOTAL DEPOSITS	41,119	41,780	34,981
LOANS TO DEPOSITS	57.0%	55.8%	47.1%
NUMBER OF ACCOUNTS			
COMMERCIAL NOTES	942	918	758
CONSUMER CREDIT NOTES	5,585	5,514	4,890
MORTGAGE LOANS	392	391	400
DEMAND DEPOSIT—INDIVIDUAL	8,048	8,021	7,724
DEMAND DEPOSIT—COMMERCIAL	2,103	2,119	2,074
SAVINGS DEPOSITS	9,433	9,365	8,684
ALL OTHER TIME	2,202	2,214	2,053
TRUST	—	—	—

Personnel statistics

	Actual	Plan	Year ago
FULL TIME EMPLOYEES	57	56	57
PART-TIME AND TEMPORARY EMPLOYEES	6	5	5
FULL TIME EQUIVALENT OF PART-TIME AND TEMPORARY	3.6	1.9	1.6
OVERTIME	$1,092	$648	$564
TURNOVER RATE (annualized)	8.8%	10 %	6.6%

Other statistics

NET TELLER[1] LONG AND SHORT ($)

Feb.	Mar.	April	May	June	July	Aug.	Sept.	Oct.	Nov.	Dec.	Jan.	Feb.
(83)	38	11	91	(10)	(271)	(209)	(143)	(48)	560	(243)	82	(86)

NET CASH ITEMS OVER 24 HRS.[2]

Feb.	Mar.	April	May	June	July	Aug.	Sept.	Oct.	Nov.	Dec.	Jan.	Feb.
2.8	2.9	4.0	2.8	4.1	3.2	3.7	3.9	1.9	2.2	2.3	1.8	1.5

1 Total in whole dollars.
2 Monthly averages in thousands of dollars.

EXHIBIT I

NORTH CAROLINA NATIONAL BANK
A SUBSIDIARY OF NCNB CORPORATION
KEY ITEM REPORT

MIDDLEVILLE FEBRUARY, 1973

Total deposits
(In Millions)

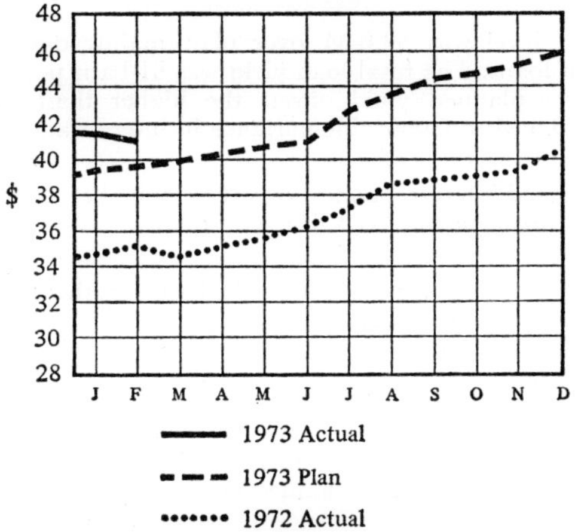

Total loans
(In Millions)

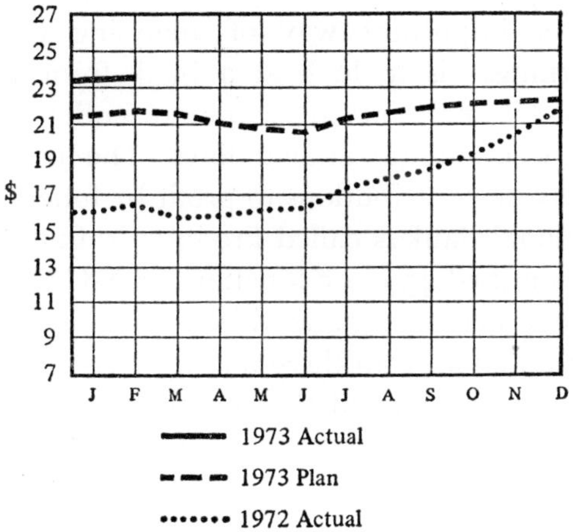

Balance sheet items in millions.

City executive comments

Deposits
The level of total time deposits was $1.9 M above plan primarily due to negotiable C/Ds being $2.0 M over plan. The rate on total time deposits was 7 basis points below plan. The lower than planned rates were more than offset by the higher than planned levels, thus causing a $6.1 M unfavourable variance in interest expense.

Loans
The total loan level was $2.0 M over plan mainly due to growth in consumer credit loans. The total loan yield was 81 basis points below plan. This lower than planned yield offsets the higher than planned levels resulting in a $0.6 M unfavourable variance in interest and fee income.

Income
Lower than planned interest income was offset by higher than planned loan fees; therefore, direct income is in line with plan.

Expense
Direct expense was unfavourable by $12.1 M for the month. Interest expense accounted for $6.1 M of this unfavourable variance owing to higher than planned time deposit level.

Hiring of an additional commercial loan officer planned for next month plus unplanned education expenses resulted in a $2.1 M unfavourable variance in personnel expense.

Equipment expense was unfavourable $2.5 M owing to payments of $3.0 M in contract maintenance planned next month, but paid this month.

MEASURING FUNCTIONS

Profit centre reporting is essentially an organizational measurement. Another important way of analysing that ultimate measure—earnings—is to look at a bank from a functional standpoint, or by analysing the services we offer to the public without regard to organizational lines. The programme by which we measure contributions to profit by function at North Carolina National Bank is called Product Profitability.

We have identified 45 basic functions at N.C.N.B. which, in most cases, cut across organizational lines, and have categorized these functions into three main groups.

First, we have determined that many of the functions deal with obtaining raw materials—which in banking essentially are sources of funds. These are the items that must be invested into other items in order to be profitable. Examples of raw materials are demand deposits, savings deposits, certificates of deposits, etc.

We define our products as the users of these funds whose purpose it is to return a profit to the corporation. Typical examples are consumer loans, commercial loans and investments.

Raw materials essentially are the liabilities side of the balance sheet, while products represent the assets side.

We also have identified those functions whose purpose is to earn a profit but which do not use funds directly in the generation of that profit. These functions, designated as services, include safe deposit boxes, automated payroll services, lock-box services and similar items.

Let's return to the organization which we previously divided up in order to achieve profit centre reports. The purpose of product profitability is to analyse the same chart in terms of functional measurement. We must again account for total income and expense of the corporation, but this time the account cuts across all organizational lines.

Using our simplified formula of the past:

The *Earnings* of the products, LESS
The *Cost* of necessary raw materials,
PLUS or MINUS *Services Income*
Should EQUAL
Income Before Securities Gains or Losses
for any period in question.

This figure in turn should exactly equal the one shown on the responsibility report—as well as that shown in the profit centre reports. Functional costing is simply another way of looking at earnings.

PRODUCTS, RAW MATERIALS AND SERVICES

We have defined our products, raw materials and services in what we term our 'product tree', of which you see an example here. You will note much more detail in some trees than in

EXHIBIT J

RAW MATERIALS, PRODUCTS AND SERVICES STUDIED IN 1972

RAW MATERIALS

- Deposits
  - Demand
    - MICR
      - Individual
      - Commercial
      - Correspondent
      - Public Funds
    - Non-MICR
      - Treasury Tax and Loans
      - Government
      - Official Checks
  - Time
    - Consumer
      - Savings
      - NCNB Savings Certificates
      - Time Open
      - Other Savings Programmes
    - Other Time
      - Negotiable C/Ds
      - Public Funds
      - Bank Funds
- Federal Funds (Net)

PRODUCTS

- Loans
  - Commercial
  - Consumer Credit
    - Time Payment
      - Direct
      - Indirect
    - Floor Plan
    - Bank Americard
  - Mortgage
  - Construction
- Investment Securities Portfolio

SERVICES

- Automated Customer Services
  - Demand Deposit Accounting
    - Lock Box
    - Freight Payment
    - Dealer Portfolio
    - Trust
    - Bond Accounting
    - Portview
    - Money Market Instruments
    - Financial Planning
  - Payroll
  - Savings Accounting
  - Software Sales
  - Account Reconciliation
  - Instalment Loans
- Branch and Teller Services
  - Safe Deposit Boxes
  - Travellers' Cheques
  - Bond Sale and Redemption
- International Services
  - Overseas Operations
  - Bankers' Acceptances
  - Letters of Credit
  - Foreign Exchange
  - Transfers and Collections

others. The amount of detail varies for two reasons, the first of which is availability of data. If, for example, total information is not available on various classifications of direct time payment loans, it is difficult if not impossible to produce output reports in great detail.

The second consideration is whether considerable detail is really necessary. Using direct time payments as an example again, it may be (and we believe it to be so) that the various loan classifications do not vary that much in profitability. Therefore, although our marketing people should keep up with the classifications for competitive reasons, its use in determining profitability would not justify the costs of calculation.

Where applicable, profit-and-loss statements and balance sheets are prepared for each product, raw material and service. Each function stands on its own. Raw materials are shown having a cost instead of a profit, and a product's profitability is shown before the cost of funds is taken into consideration.

Since one of the objectives of product profitability is to aid us in asset management, arbitrary linking of certain products with certain raw materials would distort or prohibit objective evaluation. A 'profitability matrix', which will be discussed later, is prepared which permits the matching of each product against each raw material, or against various poolings of products and raw materials. In this manner, the report's recipient can determine the impact of using less expensive raw materials and more profitable products in order to increase the spread between the two—and an increase in spread equals an increase in income before securities gains or losses.

Following are illustrative reports of a product, a raw material and a profitability matrix. Unlike the other exhibits in this paper, the functional cost data shown are not actual reports, as we feel they are of such a nature that they should only be distributed internally. Although the reports are relatively self-explanatory, I should like to mention certain key aspects.

The profitability or cost of each function is expressed in terms

EXHIBIT K

STATEMENT OF INCOME AND EXPENSE

Product E

	1971 12 months actual ($000)	Annual yield/ rate %	1972 12 months actual ($000)	Annual yield/ rate %
Direct income				
Interest and fees from loans	16,204.5	6.91	17,453.5	6.27
Income on funds sold	--	--	--	--
Fees income	--	--	--	--
Commission income	--	--	--	--
Other income	--	--	--	--
	16,204.5	6.91	17,453.5	6.27
Interest expense				
Interest on deposits	--	--	--	--
Interest on securities:				
Dealer portfolio	--	--	--	--
Interest on funds purchased	--	--	--	--
Other interest	--	--	--	--
	--	--	--	--
Operating expenses				
City main office	1,055.0	0.45	1,062.1	0.38
Branch and customer services	83.7	0.04	113.5	0.04
Operations centre	16.4	0.01	34.0	0.01
Division supporting services	316.4	0.13	392.7	0.14
Loan loss	248.7	0.11	(58.1)	(0.02)
	1,720.2	0.73	1,544.3	0.55
Other expenses				
Advertising	--	--	--	--
Profit sharing	90.5	0.04	105.0	0.04
Corporate overheads	348.5	0.15	328.9	0.12
	439.0	0.19	433.9	0.16
Total expenses	2,159.2	0.92	1,978.2	0.71
Earnings before taxes and raw material costs	$14,045.3	5.99%	$15,475.3	5.56%

Detail may not add up exactly to total(s) owing to rounding up or down.

BALANCE SHEET

Product E
($ Millions)

ASSETS

	1971 12 months actual	1972 12 months actual
Loan balances	468.600	556.600
Accrued interest	1.000	1.400
Due from banks	1.600	– –
	471.200	557.900

LIABILITIES

	1971 12 months actual	1972 12 months actual
Loans sold under repurchase agreement		
Unearned discount	2.200	1.000
Net funds used	468.900	556.900
	471.200	557.900

Detail may not add up exactly to total(s) owing to rounding up or down.

of a yield or rate—which is determined by dividing the annual income or expense by the average *net* funds provided or used. I emphasize the term net funds provided or used, because it is the *net* position that truly determines the position of the bank and the ultimate profitability of the function. Dealer reserves, unearned discount, and other factors reduce the amount of funds necessary for certain products—therefore increasing the effective yield and the profitability of the function. Conversely, required reserves, float, and so forth diminish the amount of funds available from a raw material and have the effect of increasing the cost of obtaining and maintaining these deposits.

Any servicing income obtained from the raw material functions is considered to be a negative expense. As I stated earlier, we are not attempting to make a profit from raw

EXHIBIT L

STATEMENT OF INCOME AND EXPENSE

Raw material E

	1971		1972	
	12 months actual ($000)	Annual yield/ rate %	12 months actual ($000)	Annual yield/ rate %
Direct income				
Interest and fees from loans	--	--	--	--
Income on funds sold	--	--	--	--
Fee income	532.9	0.45	433.8	0.32
Commission income	--	--	--	--
Other income	--	--	--	--
	532.9	0.45	433.8	0.32
Interest expense				
Interest on deposits	--	--	--	--
Interest on securities				
Dealer portfolio	--	--	--	--
Interest on funds purchased	--	--	--	--
Other interest	--	--	--	--
	--	--	--	--
Operating expenses				
City main office	465.0	0.39	491.7	0.36
Branch and customer services	1,145.0	0.96	1,394.1	1.03
Operations centre	1,009.9	0.84	1,386.4	1.02
Division supporting services	242.0	0.20	176.1	0.13
Loan loss	--	--	--	--
	2,861.9	2.39	3,448.3	2.55
Other expenses				
Advertising	1.8	0.00	--	--
Profit sharing	176.0	0.15	226.0	0.17
Corporate overhead	677.8	0.57	707.7	0.52
	855.6	0.72	933.7	0.69
Total expenses	3,184.6	2.66	3,948.2	2.92
Earnings before taxes and raw material costs	$ N/A	N/A%	$ N/A	N/A%

Detail may not add up exactly to total(s) owing to rounding up or down.

BALANCE SHEET

Raw material E
($ Millions)

ASSETS

	1971 12 months actual	1972 12 months actual
Float	72.000	73.600
Reserve	47.000	53.600
Overdrafts	1.700	1.100
Due from banks	8.700	7.900
Net funds provided	239.100	270.700
	368.500	406.900

LIABILITIES

	1971 12 months actual	1972 12 months actual
Deposit balances	368.500	406.900
	368.500	406.900

Detail may not add up exactly to total(s) owing to rounding up or down.

materials. Servicing income is merely an attempt to offset maintenance expense.

Finally, the income and expense categories are broken into several major classifications. Direct income is taken directly from the responsibility reporting system for the function involved. Likewise, interest expense is also obtained from the responsibility reports of the bank. Operating expenses are the variable expenses related to the volume of the function involved and are the result of allocations from various organizational units. The 'other expenses' category is basically fixed expense in which all functions share based on their pro-rata proportion of the expenses of the whole business.

Let us look for a moment at the sample reports. The direct yield based on the average funds employed for Product E was

6·27%. Processing and maintenance of the product absorbed 55 basis points of this yield. Corporate overhead and other fixed items absorbed an additional 16 basis points for a total expense of 71 basis points. Subtracting the expenses from the original yield results in an earnings before taxes and any raw material cost of 5·56% on each dollar of funds employed in this product. The sample reports for our Raw Material E shows that fee income offset approximately 32 basis points of any expenses incurred in the processing and obtaining of these funds. Operating expenses cost 2·55% or 255 basis points. Fixed and other expenses took another 69 basis points, so that when fee income is offset against these expenses the effective rate on deposits was 2·92%. Keep in mind that this 2·92% is in relationship to the *net* funds provided by the raw materials.

Looking at the statement of condition, we see that some $400 million of book deposits yielded only slightly over $270 million in available funds because of float, reserves and other factors. Obviously, the cost of this raw material can be affected by changes in expenses as well as changes in the percentage of availability funds.

If our Raw Material E and Product E represented the entire bank, the net spread on our total funds would be 2·64%. This is obtained by taking the yield of the product (5·56%) less the cost of the raw materials (2·92%), with the resulting spread being our product. Obviously, we have more than one raw material and one product, and all are shown on the sample matrix. All products are listed on the left-hand side of the matrix with the respective yield before taxes and raw materials shown. The rate of each raw material is shown across the top of the matrix. The matrix is read somewhat like a road mileage chart, in that at the intersection of a product and a raw material the spread is shown. This format of the matrix permits almost unlimited combinations to be determined in order to aid the user in better understanding and improving the earnings of our bank. Of course, this matrix does not recognize balance

EXHIBIT M

PROFITABILITY MATRIX: PRODUCT PROFITABILITY

1972 6-Month actual

		Source of funds—raw materials												
	Rate	4.51	5.81	0.84	2.33	0.85	**2.92**	7.19	5.48	5.53	5.78	5.26	3.62	5.31
Yield	Uses of Funds—Products	All Sources Pooled	Raw Material A	Raw Material B	Raw Material C	Raw Material D	**Raw Material E**	Raw Material F	Raw Material G	Raw Material H	Raw Material I	Raw Material J	Raw Material K	Raw Material L
6.83	All Products Pooled	2.32	1.02	5.99	4.50	5.98	**3.91**	(0.36)	1.35	1.30	1.05	1.57	3.21	1.52
9.61	Product A	5.10	3.80	8.77	7.28	8.76	**6.69**	2.42	4.13	4.08	3.83	4.35	5.99	4.30
10.31	Product B	5.80	4.50	9.47	7.98	9.46	**7.39**	3.12	4.83	4.78	4.53	5.05	6.69	5.00
3.31	Product C	(1.20)	(2.50)	2.47	0.98	2.46	**0.39**	(3.88)	(2.17)	(2.22)	(2.47)	(1.95)	(0.31)	(2.00)
7.24	Product D	2.73	1.43	6.40	4.91	6.39	**4.32**	0.05	1.76	1.71	1.46	1.98	3.62	1.93
5.56	**Product E**	**1.05**	**(0.25)**	**4.72**	**3.23**	**4.71**	**2.64**	(1.63)	0.08	0.03	(0.22)	0.30	1.94	0.25
5.16	Product F	0.65	(0.65)	4.32	2.83	4.31	2.24	(2.03)	(0.32)	(0.37)	(0.62)	(0.10)	1.54	(0.15)
7.22	Product G	2.71	1.41	6.38	4.89	6.37	4.30	0.03	1.74	1.69	1.44	1.96	3.60	1.91
6.42	Product H	1.91	0.61	5.58	4.09	5.57	3.50	(0.77)	0.94	0.89	0.64	1.16	2.80	1.11

relationships, in that a given raw material may not have sufficient balances to support a given product.

STRATEGY VERSUS TACTICS

Functional costing reports are not needed monthly or even quarterly. We issue product profitability twice a year, at mid-year and year end. The decisions resulting from product profitability are more strategic than tactical in nature. These decisions often take considerable time to implement, in that they involve decisions regarding balance-sheet mix and asset management in general.

An example of the use of such a system involves individual demand deposits and regular savings. Last year, there was considerable pressure by our competitors to lower the interest rate paid on individual savings from 4½% to 4%. Product profitability has consistently shown us that the so-called 'free' individual demand deposits cost quite a bit to maintain, owing to extremely high activity in the accounts. In fact, the effective costs of individual demand deposits and 4½% savings were not substantially different. Therefore, we felt 4½% money to be good, solid, inexpensive raw materials.

So, unlike many of our major competitors, we decided not to reduce the rate paid on our regular savings. We felt that the additional sources of funds we might obtain through a concentrated marketing programme would more than offset any additional interest that we might have to pay. We mounted an all-out campaign towards soliciting new regular savings deposits—and in a relatively short period of time had increased our outstandings in this category by more than $30 million. Studies have shown that much of this money was obtained at the expense of our competitors. Not only did we obtain 'inexpensive' deposits, but we also now have new customers who in the future hopefully will think of us when loans or other bank services are needed.

FUNCTIONAL STUDIES

Product profitability also has been the basis for several in-depth unit cost studies of particular functions. We have been conducting these studies for more than four years now and as a result, for example, have been able to determine the acquisition cost, the monthly maintenance cost and the cost to pay out various categories of direct and indirect time payment loans. This information permitted us to determine break-even size with regard to amount, rate and length of time for each of the classifications. Fee schedules and lending policies were adjusted where necessary, based on the results of this study.

WORK MEASUREMENT, MANAGEMENT CONTROL REPORTS

Considerable back-up programmes and statistics are necessary to produce accurate and consistently reliable responsibility reports, profit centre reports and functional cost studies. It goes without saying that inaccurate or incomplete general accounting data do not permit publication of accurate management accounting reports.

We have also found that an extensive work-measurement programme, along with its related statistical accumulation programme, is an integral part of our financial planning and control programme. Since personnel expense is the largest single non-interest expense category in the bank, the more traditional use of work measurement for headcount control is obvious.

There are, however, more subtle and perhaps even more important reasons for having a good work measurement programme. Work measurement is the basis of our standard cost system and our standard cost system is the backbone of the majority of our reports. Thus work measurement is important to the understanding of our ultimate measure: earnings. All of our branches, operations centres and most other support areas are on some form of work measurement and data collection system. These programmes permit us to determine accurately the cost of the services purchased for the profit centre reports, the efficiency of the supply unit, the breakdown of the various operating units in product profitability and the per-item cost of certain transactions.

Written and oral narrative is necessary to summarize the myriad of figures presented to senior management during the year. Primary vehicles for accomplishing this are our Management Control Reports. These reports are published within ten working days after the close of business each month and contain an overview of what has occurred during the past month and for the year to date where applicable. These top-level reports do not include the detail contained in profit centre, responsibility, functional costing, work measurement or similar reports. Rather, certain key summary data is shown along with interpretive narrative provided by our Control Department.

In each case, the comments and figures shown in the Management Control Reports are against *plan*. We do make certain presentations to our board of directors regarding the performance against previous years and, of course, our annual report to shareholders includes this information. But for internal management, the measurement is always against plan. A good job of planning already comprehends last year's performance.

The management control reports are a series of books which do eventually get into a fair amount of detail including individual profit centre reports, key item reports and other operating statistics and operational comments for both profit centres and non profit centres. An example of the type of feedback provided by our non profit-centre units follows.

Detailed reports, however, do not come out with the same speed as the summary report, as we do not wish to hold up the dissemination of information while waiting for a few details.

A final comment about our management control report

EXHIBIT N

NORTH CAROLINA NATIONAL BANK
A SUBSIDIARY OF NCNB CORPORATION
KEY ITEM REPORT: PERSONNEL

PERSONNEL FEBRUARY, 1973

Narrative Highlights

Profit Plan Performance:

In February, the Personnel Division experienced an 8.4% ($9,400) favourable variance. This resulted primarily from favourable variances of $4,900 in Personnel Expense, $3,900 in Professional Fees, $8,600 in Recruitment Expense and unfavourable variances of $6,100 in Employee Transfer Expense and $4,200 in Retirement Pay Expense.

Employee levels merit increases, and overtime:

Total bank employment increased from 3,402 in January to 3,440 in February.

Exceeding their full-time complements are Clanton, Maplesville and Lidleton because of overlapping hires and Loraville while awaiting a complement increase.

All areas remain within their part-time complements with the exception of Maplesville due to overlapping hires.

Overtime expense increased from $41,081 in January to $55,588 (2.5% of base salaries) primarily because of seasonal increases from the operations centres.

During February 75.7% of all eligible non-officers received 66.4% of the non-officer merit budget.

Other highlights and plans:

Turnover for the past 12 months was 20.5% reflecting a 0.6% decrease from December levels.

	Actual employment	Actual full-time equivalent	Plan full-time equivalent
Part-time	360	186.31	206.68
Temporary	38	10.53	9.53

programme is that the distribution of these reports is extremely limited. Few people in the organization receive all the books or even a book in total. As was the case in our responsibility reporting programme and all other programmes, we try to provide information on a need-to-know basis. Too much information often can be just as detrimental as not enough.

I meet monthly with key executives to discuss the performance of the previous month and what we intend to do in the future.

Employment Highlights

Total employees — full-time equivalent basis
(000's)

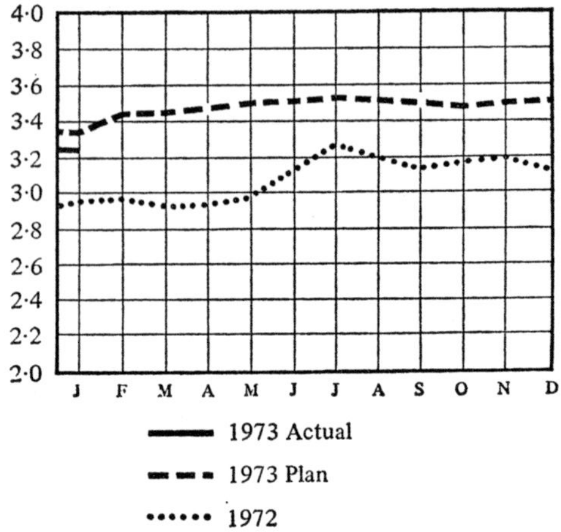

Full-time employees
(000's)

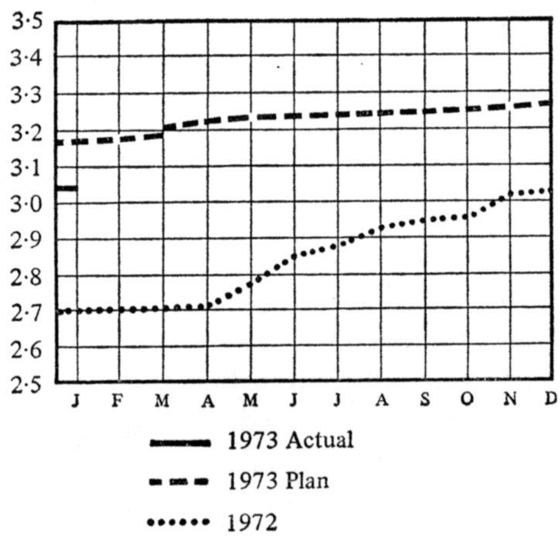

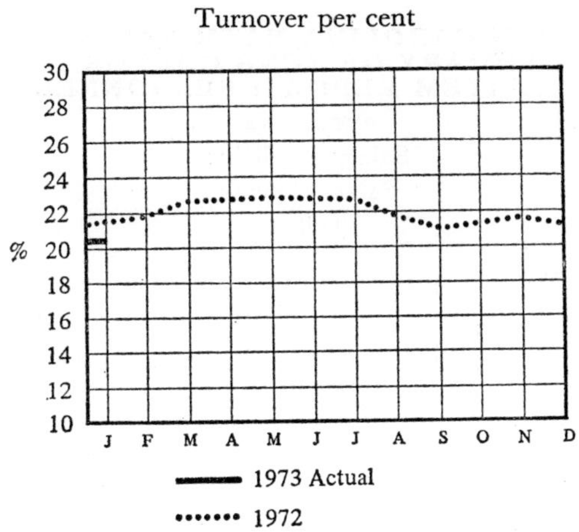

		This month	Last month	Year ago
	Plan	3172		
Full-time employees	Complement	3110	3051	2737
	Actual	3042	3008	2700
	Vacancies	68	43	37
	Plan	369		
Part-time employees	Complement	347	338	294
	Actual	360	353	296
	Vacancies	(13)	(15)	(2)
Temporary employees	Plan	24		
	Actual	38	41	57
Full-time equivalent employees	Plan	3381		
	Actual	3239	3164	2894

The basis of our meeting is the monthly Management Control Report. Thus we have taken the statistics and numbers, summarized them in a written narrative, and culminated the monthly reporting cycle with an open verbal discussion. As the net result, we take *action* to improve or to continue our performance the following month—and hopefully as long as we are managers.

EXHIBIT N

NORTH CAROLINA NATIONAL BANK
A SUBSIDIARY OF NCNB CORPORATION
KEY ITEM REPORT: PERSONNEL

FEBRUARY, 1973 PERSONNEL

Salary highlights

Salary expense

(000's)

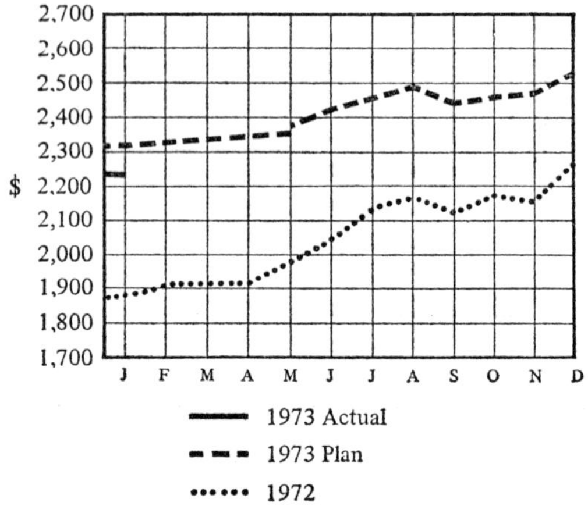

Overtime dollars

(000's)

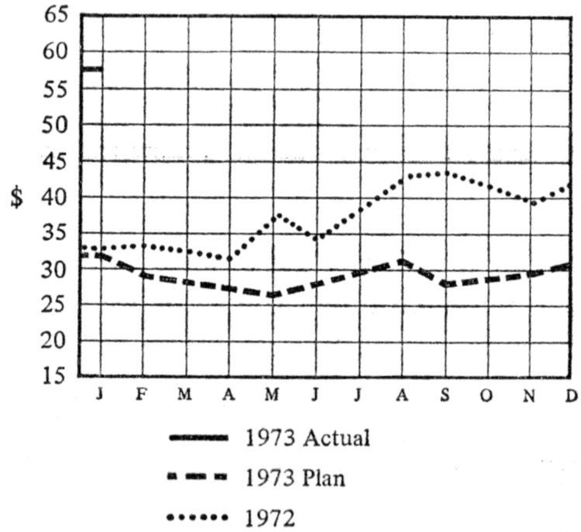

Salary expense ($)		This month	Last month	Year ago
Full-time employees	Plan	2201.8		
	Actual	2127.8	2193.3	N/A
Part-time employees	Plan	0100.7		
	Actual	0096.8	0079.8	N/A
Temporary employees	Plan	0004.3		
	Actual	0011.1	0010.2	N/A
Total	Plan	2306.8		
	Actual	2235.7	2283.3	1950.9

Salary reviews	Officer		Non-officer	
	This year	Last year	This year	Last year
Salary increase budget	$513,678	$424,910	$638,297	$562,787
Per cent of budget awarded to date	35.6%	30.3%	12.1%	11.6%
Per cent of employees reviewed to date	31.1%	35.5%	13.0%	11.7%
Per cent of employees reviewed receiving increases	64.7%	58.9%	75.7%	69.9%

Income and expenses in thousands

THE FINAL INGREDIENT

The final—or, in some ways, the first—ingredient in a sound financial planning and control system is good people. The entire system, in last analysis, is nothing but a way to provide better tools for people who manage.

It takes trained, competent personnel in the control function to produce the many reports. These people must know management, accounting and banking. It takes good managers in the profit centres and non-profit centres to provide the raw data, to analyse the reports in the replanning stage.

Conversely, a system of the type I have described is extremely beneficial to management in identifying outstanding personnel. It is much easier to spot the good ones when you can track their performance on a month-to-month basis . . . and relate this performance immediately to earnings.

To conclude: a sound financial planning and control system will improve the earnings of your company. I think you need only look at the published reports of those who have successfully established such programmes to validate my statement.

The important thing is not whether you have one monthly report or a dozen. It is not whether you are totally computerized. A good system can be anything from the relatively sophisticated programme I have described to sitting down periodically and jotting down on a piece of paper what you plan to do—then following through with the appropriate steps in the implementation process.

Our job is management—and financial planning and control are necessary ingredients to our success.

Personnel Management

by T. P. Lyons

The story of personnel management in industry and commerce is the story of what has been called 'concern for people'. Before the Industrial Revolution there was a simplicity about industry in Britain that made it unnecessary to talk about the personnel 'function'—or indeed any 'function'. Most businesses were concerned with a craft and were owner-managed. There was a direct relationship between the owner and his work people. What needed to be done was self-explanatory. The effect of an owner's decision on his employees was immediately obvious.

With the Industrial Revolution machines became the new and vital agents of production, and work people were eventually forced to combine against owners and management in order to avoid oppression. Whereas the mediaeval guilds had made no distinction between employer and employee, the new form of combination reflected conflict rather than identity of interest.

'Concern for people', however, took two separate forms. One was quasi-political—defending the growth of trade unionism and the right to strike; the other was the more personal form of respect for the individual as demonstrated by men like Robert Owen and the Quakers—Rowntree and Cadbury—who saw it as a Christian duty to provide for the welfare of their workers.

It was probably because of this concept of personal concern as opposed to political interest that the concept of industrial welfare as an intrinsic part of industry developed. Indeed, the very first organized movement in this field was concerned with the medical aspect of employment.

The dual aspect of personnel management remains to this day even within industry itself. It is possible to regard the personnel function as being split primarily between that part which is concerned with the practical and economic issues of dealing with the power structure, and the politics of trade unionism, and that part which is concerned with the treatment of individuals—the study of human nature as it expresses itself in people at work. The parts are inter-related, because both involve an understanding of human behaviour and the skills of dealing with both group and individual interaction.

Intrinsic Function of Management

It is important at this stage to point out that personnel management is not something conducted by a specialist operator on behalf of management as a whole. It is an intrinsic function of management itself. The Institute of Personnel Management's definition is useful in making this clear:

> Personnel management is a responsibility of all those who manage people, as well as being a description of the work of all those who are employed as specialists. It is that part of management which is concerned with people at work and with the relationships within an enterprise. It applies not only to industry and commerce, but to all fields of employment.
>
> Personnel management aims to achieve both efficiency and justice, neither of which can be pursued successfully without the other. It seeks to bring together and develop into an effective organisation men and women who make up an enterprise, enabling each to make his own best contribution to its success, both as an individual and as a member of the working group. It seeks to provide fair terms and conditions of employment and satisfying work for those employed.

It is important to understand that a relationship must exist by definition between superior and subordinate, and that it is the most fundamental relationship in any normal organization. It is true that there are some organizations where the sense of having any boss other than the system which is to be operated has been reduced to a minimum. Bus and train drivers, for example, carry out a schedule and are supervised in a way by the task itself. The Norwegian firm, Norsk Hydro, has deliberately developed the experiment of self-organized groups which set their own task and organize themselves to best achieve their targets. Some other organizations, particularly in the research field, use the project group system whereby the leader of any particular team dealing with a specific task is chosen solely for his expertise and in no way on account of his hierarchical seniority. Under circumstances such as these, entirely new relationships are established quite different from the master/servant relationships inherent in normal hierarchical structures in industry and commerce. However, other strains and stresses are set up because the humanizing agency of the individual manager is less available, or at least less perceptible, and the on-going inspiration of personal leadership is lacking.

Advisory Role

Rightly or wrongly, we in banking operate in a climate in which people are supervised by an appointed authority, and the supervisory role of the manager is incomplete if it does not essentially include the basic 'concern for people', which constitutes the personnel function of management.

For this reason we should regard the personnel specialist as being primarily advisory to those who actually manage the personnel and who by so doing can therefore be held responsible and accountable for their own departments.

The U.K. Commission on Industrial Relations has recently published a report on 'Management's Role in Industrial Relations'. This report stresses two things which might at first seem incompatible, namely:

(*a*) that the personnel function should be represented at the highest level of management, if not on the board itself; and
(*b*) that it is the responsibility of management as a whole.

There are those who willingly accept (*b*), but consider that the existence of a very senior functionary could weaken the sense of a widespread managerial responsibility for personnel affairs. If this were true of personnel matters, it should equally be true of other functions which it is commonly accepted should be the conscious concern of all management, e.g. finance, administration and the employment of productive resources. In practice, the argument is rarely voiced in respect of these functions. Many very cost-conscious companies employ finance directors or put their chief accountant on the board. Similarly, enterprises with the most widespread requirement for technical expertise usually have this expressed at board level, sometimes even in the chief executive himself.

High-Level Representation

The principal resources of any business are its capital, its labour and its expertise—the last being the product of the first two. There is no evidence that those businesses which regard the first two as being as important as the third have found that this has weakened the general acceptance of responsibility for those resources amongst their management. No one who knows Shell, I.C.I., Philips, Unilever, I.B.M., Ford or Glacier Metal, for example, would say that their management is any the less conscious of its responsibility for human resources because the personnel function is represented at board level. The truth is that it is because of, rather than in spite of, the high level of representation of the personnel function that personal skills and a sense of accountability for the handling of people have been inculcated amongst management as a whole.

Two major changes have taken place in all forms of working life—the armed forces, the public service, industry and commerce. The first of these has been the growing need for highly developed expertise or skill, so that being a natural leader has become an inadequate qualification on its own for management. Furthermore the natural gift of leadership is most unlikely to be sufficiently widespread to be found invariably combined with the other talents which we require in most of our managers and supervisors today. The modern services officer has to be a technician. In the U.K. the Fulton Report demonstrated that the Civil Service must be organized around the need for highly developed expertise, rather than the general adaptability of people with a 'good background' and evidence of high intellectual ability. Local government in the U.K. has recognized (in the Bain report) the need to adapt its training and education programmes, and indeed its organization, to the need for specialist expertise. Similarly, industry and commerce have recognized that, whilst still seeking the all-rounder to be developed for 'general management', management of a truly 'general' nature occurs only at a fairly high level, and the people who reach that level are likely, in the future, to have built their experience on the foundation of a particular skill or qualification. We cannot therefore take if for granted that all our line managers will have the time, the inclination or the natural ability to handle the problems of 'man management' unaided.

Democracy in Employment

The second change which has been taking place concurrently adds to the problems created by the first. The concept of democracy as a way of life, not confined to politics and civil liberties, has spread to the field of employment. The demand for consultation, and even participation, has become rapidly more fashionable, partly because it is visible in the laws and practices of some of Britain's new partners in the E.E.C.

Our laws in Britain, via particularly the Contracts of Employment Act, the Redundancy Payments Act and the Industrial Relations Act, have limited the freedom of management to be authoritarian or to base their decisions affecting people solely on instinct. Indeed, we sometimes feel a little jealous of the centurion in the New Testament because we can no longer command what we like and accept unquestioning obedience.

The task of managing personnel has therefore become more difficult both in terms of the intrinsic problems involved and in terms of the likely capacity of the average manager to cope with them satisfactorily. He needs advice and guidance in a field which is no longer second nature to most well-educated men of good disposition, and a capacity to 'get on with people'—even if he combines these qualities with the other crucial skills and expertise which we require him to have. It is for this reason that the personnel function of management, as a whole, has now to be supported by specialists, and that personnel management has become a recognized and necessary service to industry.

Social Change

Alongside the forces at work within industry and commerce which affect the problems of employing people, external influences impinge which we must recognize and to which we must adjust. These frequently come under the broad heading of social change. Sometimes they find expression in laws such as those just mentioned which are directly aimed at employers, because there is a recognized relationship between employment conditions and their social effect. These laws express a national attitude towards the role of employers and their responsibilities to society. The British government's proposed legislation on pensions is another facet of this development. Even the manner in which we finance national security benefits expresses the philosophy of a nation towards responsibilities of industry, e.g. it is still generally imagined that we are more of a welfare state than most. Quite apart from the fact that our national social security benefits are on the whole lower than those of our European partners, we currently finance them much less from employers' contributions than is the norm in the E.E.C. Compared with the other E.E.C. countries we finance a lower level of benefit by a proportionally higher use of the general taxation system.

To my mind this financially lower level of involvement in social welfare is symptomatic of a greater degree of mental detachment between industry and commerce and the rest of society in this country than is desirable.

Employment and Education

I have in mind particularly the example of the detachment between industry and commerce in the U.K. and the educational system. It might be argued that our educational legislators and the education authorities have themselves shown a lack of interest in the needs of industry, but herein lies the rub. The philosophy of successive governments since 1944 has been to maximise the capacity of the education system to develop the talents of our young people. In other words, we educate as highly as we can without regard to employment opportunities. Education is regarded as requiring no justification other than its own innate value. In fact, we have reached the stage where it would be political suicide for any party to take any other view. Occasionally, as with the Dainton Report, we recognize a shortfall in particular disciplines—in this case it was technical and scientific education which was found wanting—but no-one has suggested a reduction in output of any discipline other than to enable an increase in output of another.

Given this basic philosophy, that education should always be open to the talents, should not industry and commerce consider, more than they have done, the impact of this on them? A simple example occurs in our own industry. Whether we need their educational qualifications or not, the boys and girls that the British banks used to recruit because they had School Certificates in 5 subjects—which they presumably needed—are now proceeding at least to A levels, and, to an ever increasing extent, to a degree or diploma from technical college, polytechnic or university.

However, these now more educated young people frequently expect careers which will challenge their more developed minds. We have to decide whether (*a*) to try and persuade them that job opportunities have not changed in line with educational progress, or, (*b*) to do without them and reorganize, accepting a lower standard than that which we used to require, or (*c*) reorganize so that these young people can be recruited and provided with challenging careers compatible with their education.

Manpower Planning

Manpower planning is a complex and essential process today. The complexity stems, to some extent, from the fact that the macro-problem of the U.K.'s total manpower projection and distribution is relevant to the micro-problem of each individual enterprise.

The government has recognized the national need to the extent of proposing the establishment of a Manpower Services Commission. This body will advise the government on all aspects of manpower problems and will control both the Employment Services Agency and the Training Services Agency set up within the Department of Employment, but which will become statutory corporations. These may be regarded as a bridge between national planning and the problems encountered in individual enterprises.

One has some doubts as to whether the span of the proposed commission's influence will be wide enough for it to cover all the facets of national manpower planning. There are many problems of manpower at a national level which would be beyond the scope of the agencies mentioned above and, whilst the commission will be able to advise the government on any aspect of manpower, there does seem to be some gap in the provisions for linking this organization with industry as a whole in respect of matters other than those dealt with by the employment and training agencies. Fortunately, the problem of relating national manpower planning to the needs of the individual business is becoming widely recognized. At the time of writing, the O.E.C.D. has just set up a study group co-sponsored by the Manpower Society, the Society for Long-Range Planning, and the Institute of Personnel Management, to study this very problem.

I have mentioned one aspect of this as it affects banking, namely the effect of national education development on recruitment and career structures. Difficulties are greater because of the typical small branch structure of the clearing banks. A mobile, acquisitive and reasonably educated labour force fits badly into the needs of a business based on small units providing within themselves very slow promotion prospects and requiring stability and training by lengthy experience to meet the expectations of their customers.

Women in Banking

Amongst other ways, the banks have tried to tackle their manpower problems by increasing the employment of female staff—(*a*) because they are in less short supply than men; and (*b*) because they tend to be less concerned about promotion. They have tried to provide stability through male staff recruited on the whole from an educational level which, in these times, though unlikely to contain men of high ability, is nevertheless likely to remain reasonably settled. However, social attitudes change and are sometimes reinforced by law. Women have already obtained equal pay in banking and, aided and abetted by the law, may well come to demand equal opportunity. The requirements of top management, and even of branch management, in our competitive times, with added services and complexity, are likely to require people of higher intelligence than would normally be expected from school-leaver recruitment. The male staff which currently forms the bulk of the pool from which management is to be drawn may well prove inadequate. It is certain that the intake of young people of both sexes with higher education will have to be increased, and such restructuring as is necessary to provide progressive careers will have to be done if the banks are going to remain vigorous and competitive in the future.

Training

Training is a well-established and well-supported operation in British banking. The management of our banks cannot be accused of being parsimonious in this field. Nevertheless, in the light of what I have said about the changing social scene, the mobility and ambition of young people, and the need to recruit and satisfy well-educated men and women, there is one major change in our attitude towards training that we must bring about. We have to learn that one of the effects of further education is to speed up the capacity to learn and, whilst the need for experience can never be eliminated, it can be substantially reduced by training methods. Some banks have developed programmed learning as a means of doing this, although I doubt if its full potential has yet been exploited outside the training departments. It is, however, in the line departments that it can be most effectively used to speed up the learning process, as it is essentially a self-teaching process. Nor to my knowledge have the banks developed the analytical methods of training which have made so much impact elsewhere, particularly in light industry. In this method the actual skills employed in routine work are distilled, and model tasks are set up piece by piece so that speed and accuracy can be acquired in each piece and the pieces gradually put together to form a whole. The models are sufficiently akin in nature to the actual jobs likely to be performed at the work place for the trainee to be able to assimilate the live job rapidly as soon as it has to be faced.

Above all, I suspect that the judgment element in the basic skills of banking, as exercised in junior management, is exaggerated, the common belief being that only many years of experience can enable such judgment to be exercised. No one would deny the added value which experience and maturity can give to ordinarily competent performance. But this is not to say that *adequate* judgment cannot be rapidly produced by concentrated training using such techniques as case studies, rôle-playing, and closely-monitored exposure training. Risks are indeed taken in short-circuiting experience, but the potential loss through inexperience must be weighed up against the loss arising from shortage of staff and the heavy costs of labour turnover, caused by frustration or indeed the inability of a bank to recruit suitably, because of its reputation as a dead-slow career machine.

Motivation

Motivation lies at the heart of commercial success. The personnel policy of any organization is reflected in its style of motivation, and this is to a large extent expressed in its remuneration policy. This policy is a tool of management.

I am making the assumption that people work primarily for money. It is true of course, as eminent social scientists have observed, that there is a list of priorities motivating people, which change as various human needs are satisfied. A man needs food, and he will work like a slave to get it if he is starving. Then he needs shelter, then comfort, recognition, status and finally self-fulfilment. As he achieves each he is motivated most by the next. Money, however, is usually involved in these motivators because it is often a necessary adjunct to make the realization of the higher motivator possible. This is a point frequently overlooked. It is not only, however, the absolute value of the money, but it is also the way in which it is related to a man's work that matters. I do not mean that by paying more than your competitors you always get the best people, or that your staff will necessarily work harder for that reason. I mean that the basic adequacy of salaries, the relationships between salaries both by internal and external comparisons, the extent to which they satisfy social expectations (e.g. progressive rates) and the extent to which they reflect performance—all these provide tangible evidence of an employer's own sense of values, and also facilitate the higher motivational factors for which, as I pointed out above, money is normally necessary if they are to be meaningful.

It is interesting to look at the characteristics of the British banking industry, and in particular of branch banking, because the spectrum would otherwise be too wide.

It is institutional, on the whole, though with a history of paternalistic behaviour; it is strongly hierarchical, organized, and concerned with accuracy, reliability and integrity. It is career-structured to the extent that it expects long service and, unlike many other industries, it only starts to become technical at the supervisory level—the technique tending to increase with seniority. It is highly labour-intensive and normally very profitable.

Remuneration Policy

Not surprisingly, therefore, it has developed certain characteristics in its remuneration methods. Salaries have been highly organized but, until recently, without a systematic assessment of the extent to which they reflect the value of work being done. Salary ranges have therefore covered wide ranges of job level. Progress has been almost automatic, but steady, and at the level where most people are employed they have been respectable but not particularly high.

The 'pay slope', however, has been steep—that is to say once the routine level of work has been passed, the rate of payment for the level of work has become much higher until, at the senior management level, banking salaries, as a reward for the level of responsibility, are amongst the highest in the U.K. Variations in the rate of salary progress have been controlled by centralized authority rather than by the immediate manager or supervisor of the individual concerned. The relatively high level of management remuneration has not, however, been 'felt' in clearing banks because, with age and service as dominant qualifications, able men have often had to wait too long to reach the high-paying jobs of which they are capable.

Recently, however, two movements have taken place which have been designed deliberately to change the character of British banking *through* its salary policies. One has been the use of job evaluation for clerical staff so that: (*a*) pay is more accurately related to the economic worth of the job; and (*b*) progression without promotion is limited.

The other, though not yet universal, is the development of systematic job evaluation for management, together with provision for wider salary ranges and greater variability of the rate of progression between individuals. It is not difficult to imagine further development in each of these fields which could, if we so wished, fundamentally alter the character of the British branch banking system. The first would be the establishment of the fixed 'rate for the job' for clerical staff—with no incremental system at all; the second would be the establishment of fully variable earnings levels—although within the limits of ranges—for managers, so that, instead of thinking in terms of *increments*, managers received salaries related only to their performance *now*, to be increased only with significant and measurable change of performance level and in no way influenced by their age, years in the job, previous salary history, etc. In my own bank we have in fact moved substantially towards this latter concept—as far at least as such a change can be made rapidly in the light of both the external and internal influences which affect any organization.

The effect of the establishment of the rate for the job at the clerical level would be to attract a different sort of clerk. The rate of pay would have to be higher than the current scale minimum, so that non-career but money-orientated people would be attracted. Promotion would become even more important than it is now for those who were ambitious, but it could be seen fairly clearly that the chances of clerks rising to the managerial stream were, if not absent, at least remote. The two classes of employee would be on totally different pay systems—as is the case in manufacturing industry. Pressure for some form of payment by results system, to add to the fixed rate for the job, would obviously come in due course.

The effect of the change in management salary policy would not only be a higher performance by the more able, but the creation of a degree of labour turnover amongst the less successful because, if operated totally objectively, the system would leave at least some people making no progress at all.

The overall effect of the two changes combined would be substantially to complete the oft-discussed process of streaming recruits from the start for either clerical or managerial careers.

My purpose, however, has been, not to make a case for such policies, but rather to indicate the extent to which salary policy can be a tool of management and an agent of change.

Conditions of Employment

Conditions of employment are, of course, part of the total remuneration package. The variations possible and their value to the employee and thence the employer would form a substantial paper on their own. I would like to survey a limited number of the issues involved which seem to me paramount.

Firstly, those which are concerned with security—which comprises principally pensions, sickness benefits and terms of notice. I do not subscribe to the belief that *insecurity* is a motivation to productive work. Security, both through the employer and through state benefits, is greater amongst many of our most productive competitor nations. Germany and Japan are examples of employer-based security; and, of the E.E.C. countries, state benefits in the U.K. are the lowest overall. Insecurity of office indeed motivates men to make themselves more secure in their business, but entrepreneurial behaviour where the sack is the reward for a wrong outcome is hardly the best way to increase one's security. Intrigue, self-protection and playing safe are the more likely responses to such an environment.

For this reason, the security provided by most major banks is worthwhile and productive. In any case, legislation is tending to make security less and less of a luxury enjoyed by a limited section of the population only.

The Contracts of Employment Act, Redundancy Payment Act, the Industrial Relations Act on dismissals, and the legislation proposed for pensions, all compel much of the security that banks have always provided, and in some cases have forced improvements in banking personnel policy.

Secondly, there are those conditions of employment which aim at giving banking staff a privileged position, but which have the effect of tying them to their employer. Non-contributory pension schemes with no transferability of rights come under this heading, but will have to be amended under the proposed legislation (which is supported by both parties). A much more difficult problem is the extraordinary advantage of house purchase loans at what are now ridiculously low rates of interest. For the young married man struggling to buy his first house, this is admirable. When, however, an employee uses this facility not just to enable him to buy a house, but to live in a house which, in comparable employment outside banking, he could not possibly afford, he is tying himself, if not to his present employer, at least to the industry as a whole.

A Choice of Careers

I have commended security, but I do not commend a deliberate policy of single firm or even single industry careers. It is not only counter-productive, it is a deterrent to many of the better educated young people today who seek the personal dignity of a career built up of experience gained at their own choice rather than the paternal care of one employer for life. There are various ways of dealing with this. One is to limit loans (other than for young men buying for the first time—where it would defeat the purpose of the cheap loan) to the notional loan which a building society would make at normal interest, so that the low rate resulted in cash to spare, rather than the maximum possible house investment. Another is to eschew the cheap loan altogether and grant a housing allowance which lessens with age and seniority.

Finally, a word about share options, share purchase schemes and profit-related bonuses. To my knowledge, no research has been done to evaluate their impact when they have been introduced. They are motivators, of course, as any financial reward must be a motivator. The only arguments against them are: (i) their administrative complexity; (ii) the difficulties encountered if a reduced income occurs; and (iii) their cost. It is, however, reasonable to suppose that financial institutions want to employ people who are sufficiently interested in money to want to build up their own capital. It is therefore entirely consonant with being a bank to accept and provide in one's remuneration policy for compatible characteristics in one's staff.

Industrial Relations

Industrial relations in banking is a sensitive and contentious subject. Its proper consideration is hampered by the very narrow interpretation that most people put on the term 'industrial relations'. In banking, they see it simply as the negotiation of salaries and conditions of employment, combined with the question of which organization, if any, should represent the staff in these negotiations.

Unless, however, we are content to see the employer/employee relationship expressed solely in terms of the essential conflict of interest inherent in the traditional bargaining routine, we must consider industrial relations in the much wider context of what has come to be termed 'industrial democracy' —or to use a more European expression 'the social partnership'.

This is best explained by pointing out that a problem exists whether staff are 'organized' or not. One does not have to be a behavioural scientist to recognize the fact that, in all but the very smallest organization, there are a series of inter-group relationships—the most obvious of which is the 'them and us' relationship between 'the management' and 'the staff'. This has, of course, always existed. The main difference between 'organized' and 'unorganized' staff is that with the former those discontents at least which relate to salaries and conditions are taken away from the shop-floor or office and compartmentalized into the negotiating situation, instead of remaining to infect everyday working relationships. Anyone who has worked in a manufacturing organization going through a critical industrial dispute will know how totally unaffected ordinary departmental relationships can be. But wages, salaries, conditions, form only a part of the issues at stake. Their importance stems from the fact that money is not only, as we saw earlier, a principal motivator, but also the most obvious expression of the employee's desire to have a say in those aspects of a business which affect him. There are, however, many other such aspects ranging from disciplinary methods via job satisfaction and career structure, to product policy and ultimately the security of the business itself. The most important question of all for management to decide is whether it *wants* its staff to be interested in these things, and then whether it wants them to be able to affect them. Seen from this point of view, industrial relations is not only a question of how to cope with a demand if it is received, but also a question of whether to stimulate the demand and to organize the results.

Joint Consultation

One of the earliest examples in the U.K. of a formalized attempt to stimulate interest in the business was the compulsory establishment of production committees in the Ordnance Factories in World War I. This is often regarded as the origin of what we now call joint consultation. More output was wanted, and the workers were asked to help by adding their expertise to that of management.

Today, most of British manufacturing industry takes joint consultation for granted. It has not always succeeded, particularly where it has been divorced from the trade union structure, which has caused it to be regarded as a diversion by management from the central issue of wage bargaining. Nevertheless, the concept of 'participation' has gathered momentum in this country, aided and abetted recently by our unavoidable interest in the strides taken in this field by our E.E.C. partners, particularly Holland and Germany. In fact, the draft or the so-called Vth Directive of the E.E.C. would require the establishment of a supervisory board with a proportion of workers' representatives and of a works council under the management board for all but the smallest enterprises.

The great difficulty about worker or staff participation is the extent to which an employee can contribute expertise at a level above his own. Undoubtedly, the best form of participation is that which provides for a representative to discuss affairs at a level within which he is equipped to contribute. To make this possible, any structure has to be 'tiered'. Certainly, the direct elevation of an untutored representative to sit with top management is likely to be entirely unproductive. It is interesting that the undesirability of our few British experiments in this direction —e.g. in the British Steel Corporation—are cited as arguments against the German supervisory boards with their proportion of representatives. The comparison is invalid, however. The British board of directors is the *only* board. It supervises and manages. The Germans do not put workers' representatives on their management board, only on the supervisory board, where they sit alongside the shareholders' representatives, not to manage the business, but to represent the interest of their constituencies in only the broadest policy and in the appointment of the management board.

Negotiation in British Banking

What now is the picture in British banking? The clearing banks, by weight of numbers, obviously have the major problem. For the most part, they have to deal with two organized bodies—the National Union of Bank Employees (N.U.B.E.), and their individual staff associations. There is no 'territorial' delineation for these two bodies, and consequently negotiation or consultation either has to be by the two bodies coming together for this purpose *or* by duplicate meetings. Furthermore, they are free to vie with each other in recruitment.

The system works within the limitations which are perforce accepted. It is difficult, however, to see how any extension of consultation or participation in depth, which would necessitate 'tiering', could be developed with such a dual system of representation. The situation is complicated further to some extent by the national negotiating arrangements, whereby the trade union, N.U.B.E., sits as a single co-ordinating body representing its members in all the banks, alongside the staff association representatives who represent each their own association, although they have a co-ordinating agency outside the negotiating chamber—the Council of Bank Staff Associations. Like so many British institutions, this negotiation structure carries its own history with it, and so far it can be said to have worked. Obviously, however, it cannot work as well as it could with a team representing the staff which carried sole and plenipotentiary powers and did not reflect in its own make-up a 'back home' division of interest which must cause a constant 'eye over the shoulder' approach.

The greatest value, however, in the representative system in banking is that whether by N.U.B.E. alone, by staff association alone, or by a mixture of both, the staff are currently represented by organizations which are fundamentally industry-based. We are spared the problems of negotiating with any organization which is a 'general' union, having no specific interest in the industry. (In this respect we share an advantage with German industry, which for the most part deals with industry-based trade unions.)

Finally, I think it is important to recognize that at a time when trade unionism has become a dominant factor in the economy and in the affairs of individual enterprises, it is better (*a*) that such organizations should represent the majority of employees; and (*b*) that they should include rather than exclude senior staff below the policy-making level. Trade unions will remain powerful, either in their present disorganized, inchoate and mutually competitive rôle, *or* as Lord Wilfred Brown (and, incidentally, the author elsewhere) has suggested recently, by being given an established and official rôle as an estate of the realm on the condition that they will agree amongst themselves the wage relationships between industries and types of work which they wish to maintain. Either way, via chaos or common-sense, it is important that their counsels should be affected by the moderate and modifying views of staff such as our own—at all levels.

GROUP DISCUSSION 1

Banks' Social Responsibilities

'Today a general consensus would be that business is far too important in society to be left to businessmen...so we have to find a middle way between the demands of society and the requirements of profitability' (Michael Shanks, *The Listener*, 8 March 1973).

'In a capitalist system it is the job of managers to maximize their profits within the law but...there is a growing area where the recognition of sensitive social issues equates with a hard commercial self-interest' (Rt Hon. Richard Marsh, Chairman, British Railways Board).

1. ***The Concept of Social Responsibility***

   Business firms have always been obliged to adapt themselves to the changing expectations of the community in order to survive. As the community increasingly looks for social responsibility, bank managements have to approach the problem in a systematic way.

   Factors involved, e.g.:

   (a) international role as 'a responsible company';
   (b) national role as 'a responsible company';
   (c) participation in community affairs—membership of local bodies; local and national government;
   (d) regard for minority groups;
   (e) customers—e.g. banking hours, money transmission services;
   (f) shareholders—e.g. constraints on profits; charitable and political donations;
   (g) staff—including working conditions, profit-sharing, education and training of staff.

2. ***Social Responsibility as a Business Objective***

   Social responsibility is one of the important areas in which a bank can set objectives and achieve results.

Other areas are, for example, profitability, market standing, productivity, size.

There is a need to balance these business objectives—taking into account the changing requirements of:

(a) shareholders;
(b) customers;
(c) employees;
(d) society generally.

3. *Social Responsibility in Action*

Regard for social responsibility should underlie all management decisions.

(a) Should the co-ordination of a social responsibility programme be allocated to a specific department?
(b) Who among staff are to be involved?
(c) The role of public relations.
(d) How is the effectiveness of a social responsibility 'programme' to be judged?

QUESTIONS

1. To what extent would legislation relating to the protection of employees, customers and the community at large affect banking development?
2. To what extent should a bank operate unprofitable services:
   (a) as a national service—e.g. loans at reduced rates for industries of national importance?
   (b) as a public service—e.g. the provision of advice for customers unable to pay an economic charge for it?
3. It has been suggested that banks might undertake retraining of redundant workers (including manual workers) for employment in banking.

   Such a scheme might show no measurable benefits for the banks, but involve it in considerable costs. If that were the case, would you support such a scheme? If so, why?

GROUP DISCUSSION 2

Finance for the Developing Countries

1. ***Sources***
   (a) Multinational agencies—the World Bank group (I.B.R.D., I.F.C., I.D.A.) and the regional Development Banks.
   (b) Individual governments.
   (c) Private sector.

2. ***Methods***
   (a) 'Hard' and 'soft' loans.
   (b) Grants and Export credits.
   (c) Private, direct and portfolio investment.

3. ***Factors***
   (a) Most developed countries have accepted that 1 % of their gross national product should be devoted to the transfer of financial resources to the developing countries and that 70% of this amount should be in the form of government assistance.
   (b) The provision of such financial resources is influenced by political as well as economic considerations.
   (c) The problems faced by developing countries in meeting their external debt-servicing charges.

QUESTIONS

1. What is the role of private investment in the transfer of financial resources to developing countries, and how should the governments of both the providing and the receiving countries assist in furthering such investment?
2. To what extent can the provision of finance to developing countries tied to the purchase of goods from the donor country be justified?

3. What should the relationship of export credits be to aid and other development considerations?
4. To what extent is it practical to use normal banking criteria when providing finance for developing countries?

GROUP DISCUSSION 3

Banks/Government/Central Bank Relationships

1. ***Reasons for Control of the Banking System***
   (a) Protection of depositors.
   (b) Implementation of monetary policy.
   (c) Implementation of exchange control.
   (d) Regulation of banking mergers and take-overs.

2. ***Methods of Control***
   (a) Banking legislation—role of finance ministry/central bank.
   (b) Registration and licensing; balance sheet requirements.
   (c) Control of credit:
      (i) asset ratios;
      (ii) open market operations and interest rate structure;
      (iii) guidelines and 'moral suasion';
      (iv) direct quantitative controls.

3. ***Enforcement of Controls***
   (a) Inspection and statistical returns.
   (b) Sanctions.

4. ***Problems in Developing Countries***
   (a) Expatriate banks.
   (b) Direction of commercial bank lending.

QUESTIONS

1. Can the 'banking system' be satisfactorily defined?
2. What are the advantages and/or disadvantages of controlling commercial bank credit by (a) asset ratios, and (b) guidelines or 'moral suasion'?
3. Can the *direction* of bank lending be controlled other than by guidelines or requests?
4. How can the government/central bank enforce compliance with 'requests'?

GROUP DISCUSSION 4

Loan Policy and Credit Administration

1. ***Loan Policy***

In formulating a loan policy the general factors to be taken into account by an individual bank include:

(a) capital and reserve position;
(b) desirable balance sheet gearing ratio;
(c) structure of deposits and loan-maturity profile;
(d) earnings requirements;
(e) economic conditions;
(f) government directives and general monetary and fiscal climate;
(g) nature of credit needs of customers;
(h) management skills available;
(i) competition.

2. ***Credit Administration Requirements***

Setting up an efficient administration for a loan policy requires provision for, inter alia:

(a) a formal structure for loan approval, i.e. a loan committee and/or individual loan officers;
(b) well-defined criteria for loan approval, e.g.:
  (i) limits—both overall and for individual customers;
  (ii) standard information—e.g. accounts for 3 previous years, etc.;
  (iii) agreed basis for interpreting information;
(c) adjustment of lending facilities to customer needs through, e.g.:
  (i) line of credit;
  (ii) standby credit;
  (iii) fixed-term loan;
  (iv) acceptance credit;
  (v) overdraft;

(vi) purchase of currency at fixed or floating rates;
(vii) covering currency risks.

(d) requirements regarding the minimum use of facilities, commitment commission, etc.;
(e) establishment of loan administration officers in the management hierarchy.

3. ***Routine Credit Administration***

Credits need routine administration during their life, including:

(a) a routine review and control programme;
(b) supervision to ensure observance of covenants, etc.; collection of intelligence; periodic visits;
(c) allocation of responsibility for collection of loans in default.

QUESTIONS

1. Is there a conflict for the banks between the requirements of a profitable loan policy and the benefit of the community as a whole? Has this conflict been increased by current pressure in some countries for economic growth without social distress?
2. In assessing loan propositions, to what extent should a loans committee or loan officers be guided:
   (a) by figures and financial ratios;
   (b) by their judgment of individuals?
   Does this judgment of individuals count for more in some types of lending than in others?
3. Should the administration of loans be totally separated from the loan approval function?

GROUP DISCUSSION 5

Banks and Industry

In a rapidly changing environment the deposit banks in many industrialized countries have been developing their services to industry, and relationships between the banks and industry are becoming more complex.

1. ***General Services***

   (a) Money transmission.
   (b) Bill finance.
   (c) Short-term lending.
   (d) Medium-term finance.
   (e) Equipment leasing and instalment finance.
   (f) Factoring.
   (g) 'Package' deals.

2. ***Participation in Industry***

   Banks as large-scale equity investors in industry—bank representatives on the boards of companies—pressures brought to bear on industry to improve its efficiency—the analysis of company prospects and assessment of a company's markets.

3. ***Export Services***

   (a) Short-, medium- and long-term credits with government backing.
   (b) Advice on trading overseas, including new markets for a company's products.
   (c) Mutual arrangements with banks in other countries on behalf of customers operating abroad.
   (d) Loans in currency.

4. ***International/multinational aspects***

   How can banks best meet the needs of their multinational customers?

QUESTIONS

1. Do you think that the present banking services to industry are likely to grow, and are there others which might be useful to industry?
2. In some countries deposit banks have become large-scale equity investors in industry. Is this sort of involvement desirable, and are there any dangers in it to either the banks or industry?
3. Do the present export services provided by deposit banks need to be improved and extended in any way? To what extent should such services be provided by small specialist institutions rather than by multi-branch deposit banks?
4. It has sometimes been said that in assessing creditworthiness banks tend to adhere to a rigid assessment of balance sheets and past trading performance. What sort of organization do you think the banks will require (e.g. market research, industrial specialists, etc.) if, in future, they are to base their judgment more on a company's prospects and an assessment of the markets in which it operates?

GROUP DISCUSSION 6

Education and Training for Banking

1. ***New Entrants***
   (a) Induction courses.
   (b) Need for commercial background education—its relation to pre-entry educational qualifications.
   (c) Use of in-bank training—residential centres.
   (d) Career planning in early years—single-tiered and multi-tiered development programmes.
   (e) Transfers between branches and functions.

2. ***Management***
   (a) Modern education and training needs—the increasing complexity of modern banking. Technical education/training and 'management' education/training.
   (b) Education—training colleges, universities and other public sector institutions. Business schools. Evaluation of courses. Attachments to other industries and services. The role of professional qualifications (e.g. The Institute of Bankers' Banking Diploma).
   (c) The development of *specialists*—from within, or recruit from outside?
   (d) Management development programmes—selection of potential managers, separate career development, etc.

QUESTIONS

1. What should be the balance between in-bank training and outside courses, secondments to other banks/other industries, etc.?
2. At what age and level of seniority should potential senior executives be selected for development?
3. The increased size and diversity of business of modern banks has resulted in a more complex structure and the

need for more education and training in management as well as in banking. How can the banks provide for this side of their managers' development and how can they use these changes in structure to provide experience for future senior and general managers?

4. Should specialists (including training staff) be drawn and trained from the present bank staffing structure, or should they be recruited, already trained, from outside?

GROUP DISCUSSION 7

Corporate Planning with reference to Organizational Structure

1. ***What is Corporate Planning?***

   (a) *Setting objectives*—e.g. profit, employee welfare, improvement of public image, within the constraints of social and national responsibilities. Balance between short- and long-term goals.

   (b) *Evaluation of resources*—assessment of the banks' strengths and weaknesses. Fixing priorities.

   (c) *Allocation of resources*—management of shareholders' and depositors' funds. Evaluating returns.

   (d) Review of corporate strategy in the light of external and internal changes.

2. ***The Banks' Special Problems***

   In banking, corporate planning has to acknowledge that:

   (a) the banks' principal services are unlikely to become obsolete;

   (b) in some countries the competition has been limited;

   (c) there is limited scope for product innovation or product differentiation;

   (d) there are limited opportunities for price competition.

3. ***Organizational Aspects***

   (a) Need for strong planning function.

   (b) Need to decentralize operating decisions to maintain flexibility.

QUESTIONS

1. 'In industries where change is slow, long-range planning rarely needs to be extended beyond common knowledge of the chief executive's philosophy of management and growth.' To what extent does this situation apply in banking today?
2. To what extent do the banks today understand their environment and respond correctly to the needs of their customers?
3. 'A forecast represents a reasonable man's expectation of what may happen; a profit plan is a reasonable man's expectation of what he can make happen.'
   With so many factors outside the banks' control, is profit planning possible for them?
4. To what extent should the banks be decentralized? In large banking groups, should special-function management (e.g. personnel, premises) also be decentralized?

GROUP DISCUSSION 8

Multinational Banking

1. ***Types of multinational banking operations***
   (a) Banks with subsidiaries in diverse financial centres.
   (b) Consortia banking groups with shareholders based in different financial centres.
   (c) The 'Clubs'—i.e. consortia banking groups where there is no shareholding involved.
   (d) Branch network.

2. ***Objects of Multinational Banks***
   (a) General banking services for customer companies wherever they may be.
   (b) Ability to tap international money and capital markets, for example, eurocurrency and eurobond markets.
   (c) Term lending.
   (d) Specialist services:
      (i) leasing;
      (ii) international corporate financial advice;
      (iii) international cash management.

3. ***Factors influencing the growth of multinational banking are:***
   (a) the need to respond to the requirements of multinational companies;
   (b) desire for an improved access to the eurocurrency markets;
   (c) a desire to escape restrictions imposed on individual domestic markets;
   (d) response to competition;
   (e) the need to improve rapid international communication systems for multicurrency transactions:

(i) SWIFT—international message switching project;
(ii) international money transmission service.

(f) Problems arising from the different central bank, legal, taxation and background regulations in the differing host countries and the reaction of these countries to the multinational banks.

QUESTIONS

1. What new developments are foreseen in the evolution of the multinational banks?
2. Are the international banks successfully meeting the requirements of:
   (a) multinational corporations;
   (b) developing countries?
   What further steps should be considered?
3. Are the existing multinational banking formations vulnerable to changes in the conditions affecting the eurocurrency markets, e.g.:
   (a) a unified system of central bank controls of euro-dollar lending;
   (b) abolition of U.S. control of capital transfers?

GROUP DISCUSSION 9

Marketing in Domestic Banking

Definition of marketing:

'The marketing concept is the recognition by management that the organisation exists to serve customers, and that it can only satisfy its stockholders, in the long-term, by providing customer satisfaction at a profit.'

(Lord Seebohm)

1. ***Formation of Marketing Strategy***

Depends on:

(a) evaluation of available resources, strengths and weaknesses;
(b) identifying opportunities in particular areas and industries.

2. ***Definition of General Objectives***

Examples:

(a) overall market share;
(b) share of particular markets;
(c) desired level of profit.

3. ***Identification of Specific Objectives***

Examples:

(a) Increases in deposits.
(b) Increased lending.
(c) Improved return from investments.

4. ***Provision of Services***

(a) Identifying the demand and the customer's needs.
(b) Ascertaining the cost of satisfying them.
(c) Selecting the particular needs to fulfil.
(d) Selling the service to the customer: advertising and public relations.
(e) Keeping abreast of changes, both in demands and the means of satisfying them.

5. ***Planning***

(a) Future markets—long-range planning.
(b) Development of new services.

6. ***Staff Aspects***

Communications—explaining objectives to managers and staff 'in the field'.
Motivation—incentives, profit-sharing, etc. Support from top management.

QUESTIONS

1. In recent years, the banks have paid much more attention to marketing techniques. Why has this happened?
2. The financial and technical climate is changing rapidly today. What are the biggest problems for bank marketing posed by these changes?
3. In the U.K. the success of 'money shops' and similar institutions seems to indicate a need for a more informal approach to banking.* How widespread is this preference, and is the trend likely to continue?

* See the *Journal of the Institute of Bankers* for April 1973, pp. 71–82.

GROUP DISCUSSION 10

Developments in Medium- and Long-term International Finance

1. ***In relation to export finance, some control over credit terms is exercised by the Berne Union of Credit Insurers. Factors affecting such control are:***

   (a) greater use of the buyer credit lines rather than the supplier credit;
   (b) harmonization of export credit systems through, for example, E.E.C. and O.E.C.D.;
   (c) spread of multinational corporations capable of bidding a project from any one country or any combination of countries;
   (d) export subsidies.

2. ***Overall the current trend is towards longer repayment terms.***

   Causes include:
   (a) larger individual project values;
   (b) greater competition between banks;
   (c) supply and demand relationship in international money markets;
   (d) central controls exercised by governments of developing countries on borrowing terms.

   Factors to notice:

   (a) rapid growth of eurobond market;
   (b) decline in margins;
   (c) increasing range of borrowers;
   (d) stimulation of foreign lending to mitigate effective trading surpluses.

3. ***Government controls affect decisions as to how long-term international financial arrangements are packaged. Such factors include:***

   (a) taxation;
   (b) centralized control of public and/or private sector external borrowing, e.g. the planned economies;
   (c) exchange control.

4. ***The banks have adapted to meet international financial requirements of industry by:***

   (a) international factoring, medium- and long-term;
   (b) leasing;
   (c) consortia banking;
   (d) multicurrency options in loan agreements.

QUESTIONS

1. Is the trend towards a greater use of buyer credit in preference to supplier credit to be encouraged? Is it desirable to reach complete harmonization of export credit facilities?
2. Is it desirable or justifiable that the authorities of either the borrowing countries or the lending countries should seek to exercise control over the term of borrowing?
3. To what extent are the long-term financial requirements of industry satisfied by the existing financial techniques available?

GROUP DISCUSSION 11

Consumer Credit and Instalment Finance

1. ***Extent of Consumer Credit in Various Countries***

   Consumer credit industries in 'developed' economies—size of debt—possibility of international comparisons.

2. ***Lending Institutions:***

   (a) Hire-purchase companies: principal differences between hire-purchase, at point of sale, and bank finance.

   (b) Banks:

      (i) direct interest through personal loans, etc.;

      (ii) credit cards;

      (iii) indirect interest through acquisition of finance houses.

   (c) Building societies.

   (d) Retailers (budget accounts, hire purchase or credit sales agreements, etc.).

   (e) 'Check' traders.

   (f) Development of 'money shops'.

3. ***Government Controls***

   Over the various types of institutions—

      (i) direct, e.g. on hire purchase terms;

      (ii) indirect, on asset ratios of deposit-taking institutions.

4. ***Instalment Finance Terms***

   Structure of interest rates, size of deposit, etc.

5. ***Credit Information***

   The available sources, and value, of credit information.

QUESTIONS

1. The volume of consumer credit has been increasing rapidly in many countries in recent years. Do you think that on balance the economic and social effects are likely to be beneficial?

2. In many countries the boundaries between different types of financial institutions are breaking down: this applies particularly to the big banks and finance houses in the U.K. In these circumstances what is the future likely to be for institutions which at present specialize in consumer credit?

3. One of the tools of economic management has been the regulation of terms, e.g. the level of deposits required or the maximum period for repayment, in consumer credit and instalment finance transactions. What are the advantages and disadvantages of this type of control?

GROUP DISCUSSION 12

International Financial Centres

1. ***Reasons for Growth***

Factors conducive to the establishment and growth of an international financial centre:

(a) absence of rigid banking regulations;
(b) absence of discrimination in tax and legal system;
(c) favourable climate for international finance;
(d) developed domestic banking system;
(e) developed capital market;
(f) developed financial infrastructure, e.g. insurance, commodity markets, stock market, transport and trading;
(g) concentration of sophisticated financial expertise;
(h) political stability.

2. ***Current Trends***

(a) A number of new financial centres are becoming increasingly important, e.g. Hong Kong, Singapore and Tokyo.
(b) London is a dominant centre for the eurocurrency market, but not the eurobond market.
(c) The European financial centres satisfy the requirements of domestic industry largely by domestic banking methods.
(d) The influx of foreign banks into international financial centres has repercussions on the domestic business.

3. ***Future Development***

Factors affecting the development of international financial centres are likely to include:

(a) regional trading blocs;
(b) nationalism;
(c) the pattern of the United States balance of payments, and possible changes in existing restrictive legislation.

QUESTIONS

1. What is the relative importance of the various factors which are conducive to the growth of an international financial centre?
2. What developments are likely to influence the evolution of the present financial centres and the development of new financial centres?
3. What advantages and what disadvantages accrue to an international financial centre?
4. What is the future of the City of London as an international financial centre?

GROUP DISCUSSION 13

Management of a Bank's Financial Resources

1. ***Reasons for Asset Management***

To achieve a balance that maximizes short-term profitability while not sacrificing long-term profit stability. This means applying as many assets as possible in the high-profit parts of the business, while maintaining an acceptable lower level of assets in the less profitable operations so as to minimize the risk of short-term market fluctuations.

2. ***Main Features of Asset Management***

(a) Gearing—relationship between shareholders' funds and bank deposits.
(b) Optimum structure of deposits—demand, time, retail and wholesale.
(c) Structure of assets. The range of liquidity: cash, call money, bills, bonds, advances, trade investments, property.
(d) Government controls, e.g. economic management, protection of shareholders and depositors.

3. ***Special problems***

(a) Organizational—how best to structure the organization of the bank to optimize use of resources.
(b) Forecasting interest-rate levels and economic trends.
(c) Relationships between running yields and capital profits.
(d) Calculating cost of money (viz. the difference between the cost of borrowing and that of lending money). Problems of fluctuating interest rates.

QUESTIONS

1. Banks have always had to manage assets. Why is so much more importance now attached to asset management in some countries?
2. If banks take any short-term deposits, should assets also be of a short-term nature?
3. What should the ratio of capital to deposits be for banks? Should this ratio be left for the banks to decide or should it be imposed by government?
4. What is the desirable level for a bank's holding of government stock? Is there a minimum level below which this holding should not fall?

GROUP DISCUSSION 14

Foreign Exchange Aspects

1. ***The Outlook:***
   - (a) future for floating currencies;
   - (b) two-tier exchange rates;
   - (c) wider bands/narrower bands—the 'snake in the tunnel' experiment;
   - (d) gold's contribution to international liquidity;
   - (e) role of I.M.F. and I.B.R.D.;
   - (f) the role of the S.D.R.

2. ***Choice of currency for financing operations will be influenced by:***
   - (a) comparative costs and interest rates, commissions, etc.;
   - (b) revaluation/devaluation prospects;
   - (c) disparity of margins between eurocurrency and domestic lending;
   - (d) prudence of term lending in currencies other than one's own;
   - (e) availability of currency;
   - (f) availability of forward cover and existence of premium or discount;
   - (g) costs of conversion if required for utilization in another currency;
   - (h) exchange control limitations.

3. ***The U.S. balance of payments deficit and restrictive legislation were largely responsible for the European orientation given to the eurocurrency market. This has since led to:***
   - (a) the interdependence of the eurocurrency market and the multinational company;
   - (b) the lack of official control on the structure and operation of the market.

QUESTIONS

1. What is the future outlook for exchange parities, and what is the role of gold likely to be in the world monetary system?
2. Is lending in a foreign currency any different fundamentally from lending in a domestic currency?
3. What future developments could influence the course of the eurocurrency market?

BIOGRAPHICAL NOTES

RICHARD DYSON, F.I.B. (p. 1)

Mr. Dyson, who was born in Yorkshire, is an 'old-boy' of Christ Church, where he took first class honours in classical moderations and 'Greats'. He joined Barclays Bank in 1933 and later transferred to Barclays D.C.O.; his duties took him to Egypt, Sudan and East Africa and, in 1947, he was transferred to the newly-formed Barclays Overseas Development Corporation, of which he soon became Manager.

After returning to Barclays D.C.O. (now Barclays Bank International), Mr. Dyson held, in turn, the following appointments: Assistant General Manager; General Manager; Vice Chairman; Deputy Chairman (his present title). In addition, he is a director of Barclays Bank Ltd, and of several of the bank's subsidiary companies. He is also a director of the Commonwealth Development Finance Company Limited and a governor of Sutton's Hospital in Charterhouse, London, and of Charterhouse School at Godalming.

Mr. Dyson qualified as an Associate of The Institute of Bankers in 1937, winning the Gwyther Prize for Economics in the process, and he was elected a Fellow in 1960; three years later he became a member of the Council and in 1972 he was elected President of the Institute.

Mr. Dyson lives at Chobham, Surrey, and is married, with four sons. His hobbies include cricket, gardening and golf.

RUSSELL CLARK, F.I.B. (p. 25)

Mr. Clark was educated at Bancroft's School, Essex, and joined the Westminster Bank in 1934. He took a B.Sc. (Econ) degree at the London School of Economics while working in various London branches of the bank.

After serving as a captain in the First Airborne Division during the war, Mr. Clark returned to the bank and was transferred to the Economic Intelligence Department, of which he was later appointed Principal. After the merger with National Provincial and District Banks in 1968, he was made Economic Adviser and Head of International Planning, and in 1971 he became Economic Adviser and Senior International Executive of the National Westminster Bank group.

Mr. Clark is editor of the National Westminster Bank Review and is a member of the Monetary Commission, European League for

Economic Co-operation. He completed The Institute of Bankers' examinations in 1947, and was elected a Fellow in 1961; in 1968 he delivered a lecture to Institute members on 'British Banking: Changes and Challenges'.

He was a discussion group chairman at the I.B.S.S. in Oxford in 1961, 1964 and 1970.

Mr. Clark lives at Chingford in Essex, is married and has two grown-up children; he is a keen churchman, and music is one of his main interests.

HANS STRASSER (p. 45)

Mr. Strasser was born in Bienne, Switzerland, and served his 'apprenticeship' in a local branch of a leading Swiss commercial bank. In 1946 he passed the Higher Swiss Federal Examination in Banking with honours and then spent some years in the U.S.A., during which time he was a student of the American Institute of Banking and worked for a watch sales organisation.

When he returned to Switzerland in 1950, he rejoined the Swiss Bank Corporation as a sub-manager and became a manager in 1956. In 1960, he was made responsible for the organisation and management of the bank's new office in Berne and, having completed this, he was appointed a General Manager at the bank's head office in Basle in 1963.

Mr. Strasser represents the bank on the boards of many leading industrial firms—electric power supply, watch making, chemical, food and other companies; he also acts as chairman of the bank-owned Mortgage Institution as well as being chairman of the largest Swiss group of firms in the field of precious metals.

Mr. Strasser is married and lives at Arlesheim, near Basle. He is a member of Lions International and his hobbies include golf, fishing and stamp-collecting.

CHARLES HYDE VILLIERS, M.C. (p. 75)

Mr. Villiers was educated at Eton and New College, Oxford. His banking career started in 1931 with Glyn Mills and Company; during the war he served with the Grenadier Guards in France and on special operations in Yugoslavia—for which he was later presented with the Order of the People (Yugoslavia) and an M.C.

After the war, Mr. Villiers returned to banking as a partner in the merchant banking firm of Helbert Wagg; he became a Managing Director of Schroder Wagg, being responsible for most of the

Company's overseas activities and many mergers and new issues. He also became Chairman of three international investment trusts and a director of several industrial firms, insurance companies and banks.

In 1968, Mr. Villiers was appointed Managing Director of the Industrial Reorganisation Corporation; after three years he moved on to become Chairman of Guinness Mahon and Company Ltd, and earlier this year he was appointed Chief Executive of the Guinness Peat Group Ltd.

In addition, Mr. Villiers is Chairman of the Northern Ireland Finance Corporation and of the Federal Trust Group on European Monetary Integration. He is a past-President of the International Institute of Banking Studies and in 1971 he gave the Maurice Lubbock Memorial Lecture: 'Tomorrow's Management'.

Mr. Villiers is married and has one son and two daughters. He lives in London, but has a country home at Sunninghill, Berkshire; his main hobbies are gardening and cine photography.

K. H. Beyen (p. 87)

Mr. Beyen was born in The Hague in the Netherlands. He graduated from the Municipal University of Amsterdam with a Master of Laws degree and went on to take a Master of Comparative Law degree at the George Washington University.

From 1949 to 1953 he worked for the Dutch Ministry of Finance, Legal Department, and for most of the time was attached to the Dutch embassy in Washington D.C. This was followed by five years as a member of the International Staff of N.A.T.O.

In 1957, Mr. Beyen entered banking on the staff of H. Albert de Bary and Co. N.V., Amsterdam, and in 1961 he was appointed a manager of the Rotterdamsche Bank N.V., Rotterdam. After six years in this post, Mr. Beyen became a General Manager of the European Bank for Medium Term Credit (B.E.C.), Brussels and in 1970 he was appointed to his present post of Managing Director, Amsterdam-Rotterdam Bank N.V., Amsterdam.

He was a member of the Advisory Committee responsible for the 13th I.B.S.S., held at Noordwijk in 1960.

Mr. Beyen lives at Laren, near Amsterdam, and is married, with one son. His hobbies are tennis, horse-riding and music.

MALCOLM WILCOX, M.B.E., F.I.B. (p. 103)

Mr. Wilcox began his banking career with the Midland Bank in Liverpool in 1938. During the war he served with the Royal Artillery and on the general staff in Britain and in the Far East. On returning to banking, he worked successively in Leicester, Leeds and the City of London.

In 1965, Mr. Wilcox was appointed Assistant General Manager and, two years later, Joint General Manager; he was appointed to his present post, Assistant Chief General Manager, in 1972. Mr. Wilcox is also a Vice Chairman of the Midland Bank Finance Corporation and of Forward Trust, its banking and instalment credit subsidiary; deputy chairman of Thos. Cook & Son Ltd; and a director of Samuel Montagu & Co.

Mr. Wilcox completed The Institute of Bankers' examinations in 1948, winning the Beckett Memorial Prize (for obtaining the highest marks in the final examinations). He was elected a Fellow in 1954, and became a member of the Council of the Institute in 1970.

He is married, with two children, and lives at Sevenoaks in Kent. His interests include the theatre, gardening and overseas travel.

THOMAS I. STORRS (p. 143)

Mr. Storrs began his banking career as an office boy and clerk with the Federal Reserve Bank in Richmond, Virginia, and during the war served with the U.S. navy.

After the war, Mr. Storrs returned to the Federal Reserve Bank as a statistical clerk; he held in turn the position of Economist, Assistant Vice President, and Vice President in charge of research before moving to Charlotte, North Carolina, where he took charge of the Federal Reserve Branch. During this period Mr. Storrs was also taking master's and doctor's degrees in economics at Harvard University.

In 1960 Mr. Storrs moved to the North Carolina National Bank as Executive Vice President; he was promoted to Vice Chairman in 1967 and President in 1969. In addition, he is a Director of Black & Decker Manufacturing Co. and of Texfi Industries, Inc.; he serves as a member of the Government Borrowing Committee of the American Bankers' Association (an advisory committee to the U.S. treasury), and the Federal Advisory Council, advising the Federal Reserve Board.

Mr. Storrs is married, and has a son and a daughter.

T. P. Lyons (p. 187)

Mr. Lyons was educated at Wimbledon College and read classics at King's College, London; he took a postgraduate course in Personnel Management after war service in the Indian Army. This was followed by several years in industry—working for Unilever, Philips Industries, Ilford Ltd. and Staveley Industries (where he was Director of Personnel). In 1969 Mr. Lyons joined Williams and Glyn's Bank as Executive Director (Personnel).

He is a Fellow and current President of the Institute of Personnel Management, and was responsible for introducing a new examination structure in 1972. In addition, he is a member of the Council of the Federation of London Clearing Bank Employers and the Joint Negotiating Council for Banking. Mr. Lyons gave a paper entitled 'Manpower Planning' at The Institute of Bankers' 1972 Cambridge Seminar, and he has been a member of a committee which has been considering the Institute's future educational policy.

He is author of 'Personnel Management in the Changing Environment', published by the Times Management Library.

Mr. Lyons is married, with two daughters, and lives at Sevenoaks in Kent; his chief interests are rugby and classical music. He has been trying to play golf for several years.